PRAISE FOR
It's Time to Rise and Shine,
Inspired Authentic Leadership

"WOW! You have in your hands now, a powerful key to unlocking your future as an empowered leader! What an in-depth, well-thought out and brilliantly articulated script for walking through the process of inner transformation and self-leadership. Donna is an incredible story teller and empathetic writer and coach. Her incredible journey from unrelenting self-exploration to enlightened self-mastery is truly inspirational! This guide is multidimensional in that it can be used by individuals, groups or whole companies as a source of guidance for growing a team of empowered, inspired and inspiring leaders! Bravo Donna!"
—Julia Mattis
  Top 100 Realtors - RE/MAX Advantage Realty

"Through sharing her own leadership journey as well as foundational exercises and concepts, Donna invites readers into a process of self-discovery and self-awareness. She challenges the status quo and calls forth bigger vision, helping us all to be more inspired and authentic in our leadership."
—Alan Seale
  Author of Transformational Presence: How to Make a Difference in a Rapidly Changing World

"**This book brings face to face coaching to life!** The book invites you to reflect on the current status of your leadership ability. Through compelling personal stories and the use of the energetic leadership framework, you are guided and encouraged to experiment with methods that support overcoming your blocks and opening your mindset to authentic leadership. "
—Elizabeth McGuire
  Senior Associate Director Organizational Development

LEADING YOUR WAY
TO INCREASED
LEVELS OF FREEDOM,
FULFILLMENT
AND
SUSTAINABLE
SUCCESS...

IT'S TIME TO RISE AND SHINE

INSPIRED AUTHENTIC LEADERSHIP

*The New Perspective
for Experiencing Workplace Success*

DONNA TARQUINIO

It's Time to Rise and Shine

Copyright © 2019 Donna Tarquinio
All rights reserved.

Library of Congress Catalog Number: 2019913709
ISBN: 978-1-7340184-0-0 Paperback
ISBN: 978-1-7340184-1-7 eBook

No portion of this book may be reproduced mechanically, electronically, or by any other means, including photocopying, without the prior written permission of the publisher. It is a theft of the author's intellectual property, and thereby illegal, to copy this book, post it to a website or distribute it by any other means without permission. If you would like permission to use material from this book, please contact the author. Thank you for respecting the author's rights.

Donna Tarquinio
Sarasota FL 34241

donna@beyondstatusquo.com
www.beyondstatusquo.com
www.theinspiredauthenticleader.com

Limits of Liability and Disclaimer of Warranty

The author and publisher shall not be liable for any misuse of this material. This book is strictly for informational and educational purposes. The author and publisher do not guarantee that anyone following the book's techniques, suggestions, tips, ideas, or strategies will become successful. The author and publisher shall have neither liability nor responsibility to anyone with respect to any loss or damage caused, or alleged to be caused, directly or indirectly by the information contained in this book.

Professional Editing Services Provided by Carlene Cobb
Art Direction & Layout/Graphic Design by Kristina Edstrom Designs

**This book is dedicated to every leader
who has a vision for greatness and a passion
for becoming exceptional in all the roles in which they lead.**

- It is for the **Accomplished Professionals** who have experienced traditional success and reflect the external markings that often define success, such as the six-or seven-figure salary, a distinguished title, and life in the "win column" for an extended period-of- time. These individuals—regardless of pay scale, age or overall status—often feel disconnected and restless with a sense of urgency to experience something more meaningful, more authentic, more impactful. They desire a renewed sense of purpose, passion and increased potential.

- It is for the **Mid-Level Managers** who are on the front line of performance who understand fully how to close the gap between the desired goal and achieving the end result. They are ready to use their talents and depth of awareness to be highly effective and contribute their greatest strengths and potential to make a greater impact in a profound way.

- It is for **Working Professionals**, who have hit a physical, emotional, mental or spiritual peak in their careers and yearn for new opportunities to experience a sense of fearlessness, freedom, flow and deeper levels of fulfillment.

- It is for the **Individuals** who are fed up with traditional forms of leadership and ready to experience self-mastery with increased experiences of workplace success.

It is for all leaders, from all walks of life,
who are ready to become
"The Inspired Authentic Leader"
-a renewed state of leadership success.

Do you recall a childhood experience that is just as vivid in your awareness today as it was the day you experienced it? As a child the first sound I heard each morning was my Aunt Linda's penetrating voice as she entered my bedroom saying, "Get up, it's time to rise and shine." Her strong southern accent had a way of drawing out this greeting and making it more profound. It was her way of adding some excitement to waking me up to get ready for school. I have never been a morning person so her animated expression, big smile and the shock of so much activity felt a bit disruptive to me.

She jerked open the curtains, allowing the sunlight to flood the bedroom and my tired, sleepy eyes. I was aggravated by the words "rise and shine." As I heard her approaching my room, I felt a frustrating desire for her to stay away.

Today, I am amazed by how life experiences, at such a young age, can influence our actions and become catalysts of inspiration over time. As I've continued to reflect on the emotional imprints of the words "rise and shine," I now realize their beneficial impact. Those words influenced me and provided a strong passion for leadership, which helps me inspire others to increased experiences of success. My Aunt Linda's words were like vibrant seeds planted within me during those precious childhood years.

As an adult, I am so grateful for my Aunt Linda, who brought her loving, inspiring energy into my room every day. I now realize the value of starting the day filled with the belief that "it's time to rise and shine." It brings to mind hope, inspiration and forward movement — the perfect place to start any day, focused on creating success inside and outside of our daily rituals.

The words *"rise and shine"* have continued to serve as a subtle inspiration, hidden within my choices and aspirations. They have guided me forward with a drive to excel and a willingness to step into the unknown to embrace the journey ahead. These few words have been a beacon to my leadership spirit and contributed to the success that I have experienced throughout my adult life.

I now realize we always have the choice to rise and shine. Or, we can sit on life's sidelines like a spectator, never getting into the game.

As we begin our journey together, I invite you to consider the energy available within the words "**it's time to rise and shine**." Allow that awareness to unfold naturally and be willing to explore its true potential.

It's Time to Rise and Shine!

Acknowledgements/Dedication

I am so blessed to have a loving husband who is dedicated to listening intently to each of my new discoveries in life. I thank him for his love and patience during this journey and the hardships and celebrations that came along with my quest to become the Inspired Authentic Leader.

I thank my two sons, Justin and Shannon. They have always been my greatest teachers and inspiration in life. They continue to inspire and provide me with opportunities to practice the art of patience and to manage my emotions in the moment. They each have unique personalities that provide a well-rounded perspective on being a parent. I love them both dearly and consider them to be friends as well as my sons.

I thank my mom, who has always been a powerhouse of strength, hard work and determination — teaching me the values of quality, character and commitment. These values have served me well in creating many years of lifelong success.

I thank all the friends, co-workers and leadership professionals who have influenced and shaped my leadership presence throughout the many years of my professional career and beyond. Thank you for bringing your wisdom and can-do spirit to all our shared projects.

Donna Tarquinio is an Author, Speaker, and a Certified Executive Leadership Success Coach and Consultant. She is often recognized as a coach with an impact. She is dedicated to helping working professionals win in the workplace and excel beyond traditional forms of success. She is a strong advocate for self-leadership, self-management and building a self-mastery mindset as a platform for inspired, authentic leadership.

Donna combines her 26-year corporate career working with Fortune 100 corporations such as Lockheed Martin and Raytheon in the area of Senior Program & Executive Management, with her purpose and passion for executive and leadership success coaching and consulting. She is very skilled at working across the board with professionals who are on the front line of performance and holding a key position that requires extensive commitment and personal engagement to get the job done.

Donna is a Professional Certified Coach (PCC), and a Registered Mentor Coach by the International Coach Federation (ICF), and she earned advanced certifications as a Certified Energy Leadership Master Practitioner (ELI-MP) and Core Leadership Dynamics Specialist (CLDS), from the Institute for Professional Excellence in Coaching (IPEC). She is a Certified Transformational Presence Leadership Coach, (TPLC) accredited by the Center for Transformational Presence.

Prior to her coaching career, she excelled as a Senior Program Manager for a portfolio of multi-million-dollar information technology contracts in a mission critical environment. She understands the impact and importance of embracing strong leadership skills as criteria for workplace success. Throughout her career she has enjoyed mentoring professionals and supporting their goals for excelling beyond traditional roles of success.

Contents

Section I
WORKPLACE TRANSFORMATION FOR LIMITLESS SUCCESS

1. It's Time for a Workplace Transformation — 15
2. Exploring a New Leadership Model — 29
3. The Call to Authentic Leadership — 37
4. Learning to Lean In - True Test of Leadership — 45
5. Breaking the Traditional Leadership Success Code to Become Unstoppable — 49

Section II
SELF- LEADERSHIP

6. Embracing Self-Leadership — 57
7. The Power of Choice - Creating Your Vision of Success — 67
8. The Seven States of Leadership Success — 81
9. Exploring the Rocks on Your Path to Success — 103

Section III
SELF- MANAGEMENT

10. What Type of Energy Are You Using to Create Success — 113
11. Communication that Creates or Deflates Success — 131
12. Creative Leadership - Uncovering the Four Energy Busters — 137
13. From Traditional to Authentic Leadership — 157

It's Time to Rise and Shine

Section IV
SELF-MASTERY

14. The Power of Self-Mastery	183
15. Establishing a Self-Mastery Mindset	191
16. Six Game-Changing Factors That Determine Success	205

Section V
EXPERIENCING THE ENERGY OF SUCCESS

17. Becoming Empowered through Self-Mastery	233
18. Being Exceptional as the Inspired Authentic Leader	249
19. The Leader's Edge - Unique Formula for Maximized Success	267
20. Combined Energy of Success Transforms the Workplace	277
21. Inspired Authentic Leaders, It's Your Time to Rise and Shine!	285

Section One...

Workplace Transformation for Limitless Success

1. It's Time for a Workplace Transformation

WELCOME LEADERSHIP PROFESSIONALS!

I am so excited you're here to begin your journey to leadership mastery with me! What you hold in your hands contains the key that unleashes your leadership presence in an astounding way.

This book will take you on a journey to rediscover the very essence of who you are as an individual, as a leader and as a person with a zest for success — whether you define success as personal fulfillment, impact, prosperity, well-being or any other ideal you consider important.

During our time together, you will be introduced to new concepts that will tap into your inner wisdom and identify the key elements that speak to you. Together we will capture the core ingredients of the leadership presence that make you exceptional.

Consider this book as a VIP access for exploring, experiencing and embracing a leadership presence that is authentic, powerful and deeply impactful.

There are an unlimited number of leadership development books on every shelf in every office of most working professionals. It is totally understandable for you to question why this book can offer any new insights that are worth your time and investment.

This book was created to provide solutions for workplace success and to inspire leaders to a level of greatness that far exceeds the traditional workplace experience of today.

According to the staggering statistics from numerous industry surveys, today's working professionals are not living or leading to their fullest potential; they are leaving behind the opportunity to create and experience true measurable and sustainable success.

In a recent Gallup survey conducted, it was indicated that 68 percent of working professionals were not engaged at work. According to *The Engagement Institute's* research findings, this lack of engagement costs organizations between $450 and $550 billion annually. Numerous studies revealed that leaders are simply not using their full potential to be as effective as they could be, which results in workplace frustration, decreased fulfillment and limited success.

In another study, *The Conference Board, Inc.*, a 501(c)(3) non-profit business membership and research group organization, reported that more than half of the work force (53 percent) reported being unhappy at work. *HR Dive*, a leading industry publication providing trends in the Human Resources industry, reported that 75 percent of employee turnovers are preventable. An additional study conducted by the *Anxiety and Depression Association of America* stated that 40 million adults in the United States suffer from anxiety, and that 87 percent of workers worldwide "are emotionally disconnected" from their workplace and less likely to be productive. Another Gallup report states that work is more often a source of frustration than one of fulfillment for nearly 90 percent of the world's workers.

Regardless of which industry survey you consider, it is easy to determine that we have a workplace crisis in our country. This continued experience of limited success and low inspiration is reaching paramount levels, impacting the very quality and character of each professional's work day experience. Our ability to absorb the true impact that is being revealed in each statistic is key. The questions to consider are: Will we continue to address the same problem with solutions that are no longer working? Or will we develop new solutions that offer the ability to transform our leadership presence to be more authentic and aligned with measurable, sustainable success?

I believe embedded within every challenge resides the opportunity to create a new and empowering solution. The solution needs to inspire individuals to accept personal responsibility and take ownership of their work day experiences, creating their own vision for success.

According to an article in *Business Insider*, the average person spends approximately 90,000 hours of their life in the workplace. Add that fact to your own workplace frustrations and combine your experience with the staggering numbers of professionals who are not feeling valued nor given opportunities to succeed. **It's easy to agree that it is time for a workplace transformation!**

We can no longer wait for our next big break to feel alive again. Life is simply too short to go through our work day sitting on the side line or playing it safe in the small zone. We experience too often a feeling of being limited or a lack of true fulfillment, freedom and flow that is no longer serving us. **The workday experience needs to evolve.**

It's time to envision a new level of leadership presence that is deeply fulfilling and rooted in authenticity, inspiration and empowerment to be nothing less than exceptional.

The insights and inspirations outlined in this book are designed to be an action-oriented, transformational body of awareness. It is based on a belief that increased success can be experienced through the door of becoming an Inspired Authentic Leader, a leadership presence that is grounded in a state of self-mastery and is fueled with the energy of long-term sustainable success. Consider an expanded view of the problems being encountered throughout the workplace environment and entertain the industry statistics that indicate the real nature of these challenges. In conjunction with understanding the many challenges and opportunities that exist in today's workplace, I will also share personal insights based upon my personal and professional experiences. This awareness is combined with a lifetime of study and reflection, working with leadership masters around the world.

Together we will take on many workplace challenges that leaders face and focus our energy on three core skills of leadership success: self-leadership, self-management and self-mastery. We will experience a leadership model that empowers you to:

- Craft your own vision of success.
- Identify a success formula that is unique, authentic and measurable.
- Promote long-term, sustainable success.

After spending a good part of my life in corporate America and observing individuals who experience high levels of increased success and those who struggle and experience limited success, I developed a true passion for helping others to win in the workplace. I became impatient, fed up and extremely frustrated with watching individuals show up to work on Monday morning going through the same status-quo work experiences day after day, with little to no change, and wondering why they still felt unfulfilled at the end of their work week.

Observing these workplace challenges, I often felt like I was watching the movie "Groundhog Day" with actor Bill Murray portraying a man who repeatedly lives through the same day again and again. Too often we become so ingrained in our automated work rituals that we start to resemble the famous chocolate-candy assembly-line scene from "I Love Lucy," a successful comedy series on television in the 1950s. Lucy tried to wrap chocolate candy pieces that moved along a conveyor belt with increasing speed. She became overwhelmed and could not perform her task.

As the chocolates began to pile up, she started eating them feverishly and hiding them in her apron pockets, so the supervisor didn't realize she hadn't completed her task. Can you relate to this story in a situation at work when you felt overwhelmed, stressed, burned out and out of control? Just like Lucy, too often we experience situations in our work day that are overwhelming and keep us stuck in a reactive state instead of a planned response.

THE WORKPLACE DILEMMA

From my perspective, today's work environments are filled with false workplace personas. They are filled with working professionals who have lost their passion and commitment to experiencing greatness. We have become a society that is focused on settling for the status quo and too often demonstrate a willingness to settle for a principle that "good is good enough." **We no longer have a vision for being great.** We have lowered our standards for workplace experiences and become accustomed to trading our ideas and hours for unfulfilling work lives. Our focus is now on producing quantity instead of quality, simply to hit the numbers at the end of the work week. We have shifted our awareness away from the many indicators that outline the true cost of leading from a status quo state of success.

Too many of today's leaders have disconnected from their core values and true innate talents and tendencies to become a robot-like figure who tries to fit in, comply, settle and become someone other than who they truly are. Collectively, we have forgotten who we are at our core, and we are confused about what's most important. We are trying to create success from a status-quo leadership perspective, one that is limited and simply copes to get through the end of the work day, work week or work year. Can you relate?

Your immediate response might be to say, "Oh, that's nonsense. Everyone knows they have to play the game, to be whatever they are expected to be in order to push through to the next level." Is this your response? What if, for a moment, you considered the opposite of that belief and determined that you have much more success-producing potential when you embrace higher states of leadership success?

What if we take a moment and put on a new lens of perspective and consider a new empowered workplace? It is filled with Inspired Authentic Leaders who are committed to creating success from:

- A place of true power

- Aligning core values that drive every action and outcome

- Fueling leaders with the energy of greatness and momentum to experience authentic success.

Can you invite this vision to unfold in the corners of your imagination? What happens as a society if we dare to reestablish and reshape our beliefs about the workplace experience? What might be possible?

Currently, most leaders show up to the workplace wearing their self-created façade that was fabricated as young adults. That's when they began to identify top colleges based on industry stats, parental influences and society pressures that influenced their decisions to be the best. Instead of listening to their own inner guidance and hearts' desires to create work they love or work they feel passionate about, they follow the money and align themselves with the best opportunity to play the bigger game.

As parents, we all too often influence our children's natural tendencies and set the expectations for our children to be high achievers — doctors, lawyers, accountants or other highly paid executives. But what happens if the young adult isn't naturally programmed to fit the tendencies of these roles?

Yes, of course, these individuals can take the necessary classes and go the extra mile to being accredited by a world-renowned institution. Perhaps they can show up to work and do the tasks at hand. In fact, there are many working professionals who have successfully managed to fulfill their career expectations and currently reside in a role that doesn't naturally align with their true nature. The real question is, what is it costing them? What is the true quality of their lives? Do they spend the majority of their work day trying to create experiences that rid them of their pain? Do they spend their energy yearning to experience a new passion that is better aligned with their true nature?

I believe this is the true challenge we all face in the workplace today. We have focused our energy, time and resources on creating a false workplace persona and have forgotten who we are at the core of our true nature. We each have unique qualities, characteristics and gifts that are innately alive, fueled with passion and skilled to take on even the deepest challenges in life. Just like the acorn is hard-wired and pre-programmed in its DNA to become an oak tree, the small seed doesn't question its potential or try to become a willow tree instead of an oak tree. It stays true to its nature.

Unfortunately, as humans we have pre-defined ideas of whether something is good or bad, desirable or undesirable. These notions can lead us away from embracing our true nature's gifts and potential. This is the beginning of the false workplace persona, as we start to establish a preconceived ego that prevents the natural flow of our connection and associations with our own true state. This true state contains everything we ever hoped to experience, such as fulfillment, passion, inspiration, creativity and so much more. This is an empowered state that I call the Inspired Authentic Leader, a leadership presence that embraces the leader's true nature and creates authentic success from internal awareness combined with external action.

Once we take on the role of the false workplace persona and begin to wear a mask that represents something other than who we truly are, we begin to live from a character role that others expect to encounter. Each new experience creates a new layer of details and refinement, showing the world that we have become this fabricated persona.

Consider this question: What happens when you arrive home at the end of the work day and retire this false persona mask? Do you begin to feel empty, disconnected and unfulfilled?

Each time you notice an inner desire to do something different and you respond by picking up the false mask you wear to start another workday, you are settling for the status-quo work life.

You are living and leading from a place of limitation and lack of your greatest potential to experience true success. Although, you may be riding high in the corner office making the big bucks with the distinguished title, what is it truly costing you? Leading from a status-quo perspective isn't fulfilling, it does not inspire your passion and most likely thwarts your purpose for greatness.

Now that we have explored the work day dilemmas, I'm going to propose a new concept for leadership success. I believe the opportunity exists for us to stop playing small and become empowered leaders who experience both internal and external success.

It starts with the idea that we are all leaders, regardless of your title, pay grade, position or any other self-proclaimed label. Each person is a leader by default. We are leaders of our own lives with the ability

to decide who we are and who we want to become. This is the first layer of transforming the workplace to become more productive and fueled with authentic success.

During our time together, my goal is to take you on a journey to experience two primary objectives:

1. Inspire leaders in every role within the workplace to become Inspired Authentic Leaders, demonstrating a state of self-mastery that unleashes a profound presence and a power that is unstoppable.

2. Transform the workplace experience to become a place of artistry, impact, contribution, connection with deeper levels of personal freedom and fulfillment.

These experiences are both centered upon the internal qualities of success that we have put on the back burner for way too long.

THE JOURNEY AHEAD

The personal experiences shared in the following pages were gleaned from working among the highest caliber professionals from many walks of life — including executive leadership professionals, mid-level to senior management, advanced engineers, technical gurus, masters at business development and so many others. I have a personal connection and related experience working with both struggles and victories that take place inside and outside the realm of workplace success.

Throughout my career, I became a keen observer with a strong curiosity about why some people struggle and others excel. I noticed a vast difference in leaders who embrace their work life and take personal ownership of their work day success — and leaders who leave their experience of success to fate.

Considering the impact of both the industry statistics and my own personal experience in many years as a leadership professional, I believe now is the time for bold action — to identify what's no longer working and why workplace experiences have become so unfulfilling.

Now is the time to call forth a greater vision for leadership success that I have defined as the *"Inspired Authentic Leader."* This leadership experience empowers you to craft your own vision of success and identify a success formula that is authentic and unique to you. It is measurable, sustainable and filled with the energy of maximized success. This is a leadership experience that tests your leadership skills, requiring boldness and bravery to step into the unknown to discover who you truly are. This journey will call out the primary values that influence your leadership focus and fuel you toward the success you deeply desire.

Experiencing the Workplace

Just like many professionals, I have achieved traditional success in the corporate environment. I know what it's like to struggle and to win, to feel frustrated at times and effective at other times. My career of more than 26 years has been a true test to my leadership skills and a model that has transformed me into the leader I am today.

My career started as a Customer Service Representative with General Electric Corporation for a computer terminal installation contract. It was a high-profile job, and I was happy to be given the opportunity at such a young age. I worked with several distinguished clients, customers and engineering team members to ensure that mission-critical networks were fully operational. This leadership role was outside my comfort zone at first, but each day I reminded myself of the inner strength, drive and determination that had contributed to my success in previous situations. These experiences helped me stay focused on creating value and moving forward. This role opened the door to many opportunities to experience leadership.

As my career began to unfold, I found myself in leadership positions for several Fortune 100 companies such as Raytheon, Lockheed Martin and others. Working my way from becoming a System Administrator, to Project Manager, Senior Program Manager, Capture Manager to Portfolio Manager responsible for the success of several multi-million-dollar contracts. Each experience provided great insight, inner perspective and real-world tests of what leadership is all about. I was in the midst of the corporate madness, which required an increased ability to manage my own leadership skills while simultaneously managing the 100-plus team of program managers, project managers, engineers and support team members, who were assigned to the contracts I managed.

While working my way up to an accomplished leadership role, I encountered experiences of both success and challenges along the way. For example, I felt isolated as a woman on a team of mostly men and chose not to partake in office politics. I often felt like an island of one during business trips, and I was routinely requested to take on the tough assignments to ensure the program's success. Despite these obstacles, I also experienced enormous levels of success and was respected by others for my sense of purpose, passion and the increased potential that I brought to the work day experiences.

Over the course of my career, I discovered several key aspects of leadership that contributed to greater levels of success, which I will now share with you.

Self-Leadership

- The ability to balance and manage my energy so that I could maintain my momentum throughout the day
- To understand the primary values that lived behind each leadership choice I made
- To ensure that my leadership approach was defined by both internal awareness and external action
- To embrace the ability to step outside the box and ask, "What wants to happen?"
- To embrace a mantra or inspirational mindset that guided my actions forward

Team-Leadership

- To respect every person I encountered, knowing they all had something unique to contribute

- The realization that if we were to succeed as a team, I had to get their buy-in, identify their passion and allow them to lead as well as follow

- To create a sense of spirit for the value of excellence and a desire to be exceptional individually and collectively as a team

- To instill inspiration, creativity and flexibility combined with focus, drive, dedication and a vision for success

These key aspects of leadership served me well in managing my own performance as a leader and achieving yearly exceptional performance awards. The team of leaders that I managed also experienced high levels of success and performance ratings that resulted in increased business and company profits.

Opportunities like these bring out both strengths and weaknesses of a person. Having daily experiences that test your ability to lead is what shapes and defines you. It takes you outside your comfort zone and allows you to grow, excel and become a leader with influence — **a leader fueled by the energy of success.**

Raising the Bar for Workplace Success

Embracing the energy of success is a strong part of my mission both personally and professionally. My goal is to raise the bar for increased levels of fulfillment and inspire others to make more of an impact, both in their work days and in their lives. I invite you to join me to start a workplace transformation that inspires every professional to move beyond the status-quo workday rituals and to embrace a new vision for workplace success. It's time to shift your perspective from traditional leadership to becoming an Inspired Authentic Leader who is fueled by a renewed zest for authentic success.

I have poured my passion and purpose into the pages of this book to ignite a spark within you that transforms your work day, your work life and your long-term career. My goal is to uncover the path to Inspired Authentic Leadership, a new state of leadership that is deeply fulfilling, rooted in authenticity and defined by your ability to choose a presence that evokes a state of self-mastery.

During our time together, I will share the many insights I discovered on the journey from self-leadership to self-mastery. I offer these insights as a road map for experiencing true sustainable success. You will have access to years of knowledge learned from leaders around the world — along with tools, technologies and insights valued at thousands of dollars. These combined resources will support you in experiencing your own version of true leadership success. I hope the renewed wisdom you gain will transform your work life, fueling it with everlasting potential.

As you read each chapter, simply allow the information to unfold with ease and compassion. This book is designed to transform the workplace experience and create deeper levels of fulfillment by bridging internal awareness with external success. The holistic or "whole" perspective on leadership success will leave you feeling alive, on fire, transformed and wanting more.

2. Exploring a New Leadership Model

Why do we need a workplace transformation?

Today's workplace is filled with leaders who have spent a lifetime getting the education and necessary connections required to follow a well-defined path to workplace success. They have successfully discovered the right sequence and formula for creating measurable success focused on external, tangible goals. However, at some point in most leaders' careers — regardless of age, pay scale or status — they wake up one morning feeling disconnected, less interested and yearning to experience something that feels more real. Regardless of success, leaders often reach a physical, emotional and spiritual peak in their careers when they step back and ponder, "Is this all there is?"

They yearn for new opportunities that promote deeper levels of fulfillment. They often desire a work life that is filled with more purpose, passion and a desire to contribute in a more meaningful way. In my work as a Leadership Success Coach, I often hear clients describe their longing with comments like the following:

- My view and values of leadership success simply pivoted to a new direction.

- One day, I woke up and started to feel somewhat numb, restless, disconnected, less interested, and yearning to experience something more.

When clients begin to work with me, they often are not sure how to define what "something more" truly means. This discovery becomes a part of the client's journey and opens the door to their own unique experience to authentic leadership success. What I've discovered in my work with clients and through my own personal journey, is that a time comes at all levels of success when the spirit is no longer fulfilled. The body feels burned out, and the emotions are yearning for a sense of freedom, expression and greater creativity.

This new awareness begins the process of uncovering your true potential to experience the way of the Inspired Authentic Leader. This new level of leadership is about getting real, being authentic, empowered and inspired with the purpose to make a greater impact. Does that sound like you?

I understand the intensity of this calling. I also know the confusion it brings while deciding whether to continue the path of success you've worked so long to create or to answer the call of your desire to experience a work life that is more authentic, fulfilling and deeply profound.

Embracing Mastery as the New Leadership Model for Success

Becoming a leader is the most crucial choice you can make. It is the decision to step beyond the barriers of limited success to experience a true connection with authenticity, contribution and limitless potential. It is the opportunity to uncover the illusion of self that is expressed each day, hidden behind the many masks of success and the countless badges worn to prove your value and mark your own sense of identity. Leaders today are yearning for opportunities to tap into the authentic nature that is inherent in all of us. They naturally have a vision for leadership mastery, as it speaks to their souls and defines the qualities they aspire to become.

The wisdom of leadership mastery is ingrained in each individual and often buried deep beneath the surface of success. In moments of stillness, you will realize that a more empowered part of you waits to unfold and step forward to play a more authentic game. This deep realization of your potential fuels you to step beyond the status quo to become exceptional.

We have never needed authentic leadership as much as we do now. In today's often stressful work environments, we need leaders who are empowered and inspired to take personal responsibility for their life's success inside and outside their work day.

The authentic path to leadership is an ongoing journey. It is not a cookie cutter solution, or a one-size-fits-all approach to greatness. It is a true path of personal discovery, which requires determination, commitment and willingness to let go of the destination and become a master of each moment of your journey.

Our traditional approach to leadership is no longer the path for leaders who aspire to create a greater impact. Collectively, we acknowledge the need for deeper inner fulfillment and yearn for a greater sense of freedom, expression and authentic success. Using our awareness to embrace a state of leadership mastery is the new mode of operation for leaders who are ready to transform their work into an expression of their true calling.

Although our values each differ, our shared mission is to be exceptional, the best version of ourselves as an Inspired Authentic Leader. We are open to each day, inviting new opportunities with a willingness to step outside the proven pathway and venture into the unknown. This is a call to greatness, an opportunity to lead ourselves and others to higher levels of fulfillment and sustainable success.

Do you relate to this call to leadership mastery? This is an invitation to embrace a new form of authentic leadership that includes the learned skills, traits, and years of experience you've worked so hard to craft. These skills are now combined with bridging authenticity and calling out the inner skills of awareness that have been hidden beneath the surface, waiting and wanting to be expressed. There comes a time in everyone's journey when these inner skills can no longer remain silent. They soon rise to the surface with great force, demanding to be heard.

From the seed of a simple yearning for something more grows a sense of urgency, a sense of greater knowing and a renewed inner calling.

Most leaders can remember the moment in their careers when they sensed this inner awareness and knew there were big decisions to be made. The options are: continue the same leadership path of playing it safe or embrace and partner with this new awareness, stepping beyond the traditional boundaries of success to explore authentic success.

DEFINING AUTHENTIC LEADERSHIP

At this point in our exploration, it makes sense to define leadership for the purpose of our work together. Consider leadership as a process in which we successfully influence and motivate ourselves and others to reach desired outcomes. It is the interaction that is key, how you interact with yourself and with others around you.

Leading is the way we move ourselves and others into positive action. The question is not if we are a leader, but HOW WELL do we lead?

Authentic leadership is leading through action, which requires movement to transform our capacity to lead from one state to another. Does that resonate with you? If not, take a moment and ask yourself, "What does the word 'leadership' mean to me? How do I experience it in my life today?" If you have difficulty coming up with a concept that speaks to you, give yourself a few moments and allow the ideas to flow. Try brainstorming and writing down all the words, ideas and images that come to you. Ask yourself, "What is leadership? What does leadership mean to me?

Now that we have visions of leadership that speak to us, we're ready to embark upon our journey together to uncover, explore, question, and observe our deeper awareness. Our goal is to identify the core elements necessary to experience more meaning and purpose in our leadership presence.

No journey is adventurous without having a few questions in the forefront of our minds that we want to answer. Valuable questions in the search for leadership greatness are:

- Who am I as a leader?
- What do I want?
- Why do I want it?

Although these questions may appear to be elementary, I ask you to be patient and give them a chance. Allow them to unfold in your mind like new fern fronds that unfurl as they grow in meadows in the spring. This journey is about stepping back to listen and observe, pausing to capture awareness about yourself that may have never before come to light. With a little reflection, you will find wisdom that supports you in moving forward with great meaning and momentum.

Now grab your favorite notebook and spend a few minutes noting your responses to the above questions. This book is designed for interaction, so make sure you play along to capitalize on your investment. Exercises are provided throughout each chapter, with each chapter building on the previous one.

- Who am I as a leader?

- What do I want?

- Why do I want it?

Welcome Back!

Now that you are starting to put some thoughts, words, emotions and images around who you are as a leader, and what you want to experience in your leadership presence, you might have also identified ideas on why you want it. The awareness that unfolds will continue to evolve as you work through this book.

Most people view leadership as a position of authority or a position that is held most often in a corporate environment. However, leadership is a mindset or a process that inspires action. When we look at leadership from this perspective, we realize that we are all leaders. We are leaders in our own lives, leaders in our families as parents, spouses, sons and daughters. We are leaders in our communities as community workers, volunteers, sports coaches, youth group leaders and more. Regardless of the role we play, we serve in some type of leadership position. We are each responsible for making decisions that will impact the outcome of our life's success.

As we focus our energy toward the vision of leadership mastery, I'd like to share my story with you because it offers valuable insight into developing authentic leadership qualities and provides a deeper insight to why I feel qualified to share my advice and guidance on becoming the Inspired Authentic Leader. I believe my professional accomplishments and leadership studies combined with specific leadership life experiences have equipped me with a unique leadership perspective. The combination of extensive study and successful leadership experience, both in the workplace and in my personal life, qualify me to serve as your trusted guide on this journey to experiencing limitless success.

My life as a senior leadership professional supporting high visibility clients in a high impact environment was a great success. On the outside looking in, life could not be better. I wore six badges attached to my lanyard worn around my neck, which signified my value to clients, to the company I worked for and to myself as a contributor. I achieved the desired six-figure salary, the unlimited benefits with stock options, bonus awards, the prestigious title, the desired office and so much more. My life appeared to be on track and moving forward to increased levels of success.

In the midst of experiencing my greatest success, everything changed. I was at the end of a two-year assignment following an intensive leadership training course that was filled with extensive study, homework and stretch assignments, while simultaneously functioning in my role as a Portfolio Sr. Program Manager. I was also assigned as the Capture Manager for a hundred-million dollar "must win" proposal. These efforts ran concurrently, often requiring extensive focus and dedication during holidays, weekends and plenty of late nights. I thought to myself, "No problem, I've got this."

I was known to be a high achiever who was driven — a professional with a passion for getting things done. This challenge was no different. I chose to dig in, put my head down and my big-girl pants on, fully focused on building a winning team around me. Our team members were all connected, centered and committed to achieving success. We were ready to demonstrate our individual and collective leadership abilities and make the impact required to propel our shared mission forward.

At the end of this period, I graduated from the two-year leadership training course and received the associated credentials. I continued to manage the portfolio of contracts with high customer ratings and increased sales with new work being added to our contracts, based on client trust. Equally important, we were selected as the winning bid for the $102-million dollar "must win" contract, based on the highest caliber proposal submitted. Life simply could not have been better!

3. The Call to Authentic Leadership

After the proposal selection and award, I realized how exhausted and depleted I felt. I realized the importance of maintaining balance and knew that I had pushed myself beyond my own set point for well-being. I took time to step back and reflect on what I had recently experienced. I anticipated feeling a sense of accomplishment and passion for upcoming projects, but instead, I felt a deep inner calling that stopped me in my tracks. I realized that although the recent wins were fulfilling, they didn't reflect the leadership that my spirit was yearning to achieve. There was this strong inner pull of awareness to explore something more. This vision of my desire included a leadership presence that was more authentic, more deeply connected and fulfilling. I called this awareness of leadership an experience of becoming the Inspired Authentic Leader.

From that day forward, I began to look at leadership from a new perspective. I realized that it's somewhat less challenging to be a successful leader when you have the support of a highly qualified team assisting you. The question that continued to haunt me was, "How well would you lead yourself forward on an island of one?"

How well would I perform as a self-leader when the going gets tough, when forced to lead from the unknown, and what skills would I master if I became the sole leader of my own success? I continued to ponder this question and many more over the next five years of my career. I kept one foot firmly planted inside the boundaries of my corporate role continuing to build upon my success. The other foot began to explore the potential role of becoming an Inspired Authentic Leader.

As this indecision about staying in my corporate role or exploring this new state of leadership continued to haunt me, I found myself in a very difficult and scary place. I was terrified to risk the security of my paycheck and all the benefits I worked so long to obtain. At the same time, I longed to explore this new notion of self-leadership. What would my family say? What would my coworkers think of me? What if I fail? What if I can never get another job again? What if I deplete my savings? The questions ran rampant through my mind.

> *"Mastering Others is Strength,*
> *Mastering Yourself is True Power"*
> *– Lao Tzu*

The previously mentioned inspirational quote by Lao Tzu became a pivotal point in my career, and it sums up my feelings on the day I decided to take the leap. I knew that I had a choice to make. I could either stay in the safety net of a secure leadership role or I could take the leap and uncover the path to this new desired state of self-leadership.

I had reached a plateau in my career when the external rewards were no longer fulfilling, and I yearned for a real sense of purpose, passion and to get real about my true potential. I felt the strong inner desire to uncover my true self. I realized that I needed to rediscover what true leadership was all about, if I was truly serious about being an empowered leader.

Finally, the day came when I knew that I could no longer quiet the inner calling that was pushing me to take the leap. I vaguely realized this journey was going to be a leadership experience that tested the very fabric of my being.

A few days later, I submitted my resignation letter. It was received with shock and many questions. No one could believe that anyone would risk this type of bold move, especially in the midst of their greatest career success. I was shocked, too, by my own boldness and willingness to "lean in" to whatever was coming next. As I shared my desire to step back and explore leadership from a new perspective, I was asked to take a one-year sabbatical before submitting my resignation. This request seemed like a win-win for me and for the people and projects I supported. The papers were drafted, the duties were all reassigned, and I began my new journey of discovering me. I arrived home feeling exhilarated about making my decision and anticipating the exciting journey ahead. I unpacked boxes of accolades, awards and hung up my lanyard with the six badges attached.

As time passed, I began to struggle to find my new sense of self-worth, my new identity. I explored the deep thought-provoking questions:

- "Who am I?"
- "What is my purpose?"
- "Why am I here?"

Shortly after I left my secure corporate position, the economy crashed without warning. It was 2008, and fear was alive and lingering in people's faces. My own sense of fear was numbing and seemed never-ending. I had met my inner critic face to face. That critic seemed to be shouting loud and clear: "Look what you've done! What will you do to survive? What if you don't have enough savings to sustain you?" And so much more. This endless loop of negative thinking continued toward its non-stop destination of self-pity and self-destruction.

After some time, I began to settle in and rise up, remembering a core principle that had served me well for many years. That core principle is: "failing is not an option." This was a mantra that I lived by and shared with other leaders in the corporate world; it had served me well during times of crisis. Even in the midst of highly distinguished large-scale events that seemed daunting, I invited my team to use this mantra to propel our success. Now was the time to return to the energy and inspiration of this mantra so I could move beyond my current emotions.

As I continued to explore options, I asked "What wants to happen in my life?" I finally decided to embrace my childhood desire for designing with flowers. I knew this quest was a diversion that greatly departed from my career strengths, but I was willing to try new skills, dust off hobbies and explore areas of passion that had been buried for way too long. I grew up playing in nature and remembered how much I felt alive and rejuvenated by the beauty of flowers. This quest was designed to springboard my passion and provide the space for me to feel alive and connected once again.

I took a series of advanced design classes with several masters in floral design, and I learned the necessary skills to attract the right opportunity. Soon after the training ended, I searched for high-end floral artists to partner with and offer my support. Finally, life seemed to be settling down and making more sense. I was starting to develop a routine of normalcy and a willingness to explore this new potential of creativity, inspiration and self-leadership. After a few months, this short sense of security and the world as I knew it, fell apart and my life was turned upside down.

It was a cold day in the streets of Washington, D.C., and I was working with a well-acclaimed floral artist to design holiday décor in an historic home once lived in by George Washington's brother. We spent several hours garnishing the large tree, hanging outside lights, placing wreaths and adorning the home with all the finishing touches. It was a wonderful day filled with lots of Christmas cheer.

Driving back to the design studio, we felt a little tired but completely fulfilled. The design projects were complete, and the holiday décor looked simply amazing. Moments later, the vehicle that we were traveling in was struck by a car that had not stopped at the busy intersection's traffic light. Our vehicle was struck from both the driver and passenger sides, sending it spinning out of control until it crashed into a large tree. Thankfully, everyone was alive and appeared to be okay, but shaken.

Within a few seconds, I began to feel enormous pain pulsing through my entire body. I looked down and saw that my arm was snapped in two and dangling; both wrists and multiple fingers appeared to be broken with compound fractures. My body began to shake profusely, as I looked around and saw the darkness of the winter sky and felt the coldness pouring in through the vehicle's broken windows.

Immediately, I felt the inner strength and calmness of my "inner leader" take control. I asked for someone to call my husband and inform him of my injuries. I did not panic. I knew I was close to going into shock, as my body started to tremble and jerk all over, but I had to stay focused. My leadership skills truly served me and never disappointed me during this time of chaos. In tremendous pain, I stayed alert, responding to the trauma team while they assessed my injuries. I quickly realized this unbelievable accident was going to be one of the most challenging times I had ever known. As I arrived at the emergency room, I was greeted by the hospital's trauma team of doctors, and I listened closely to them. They were somewhat intrigued by the results of my x-rays, showing compound fractures in both arms, fingers and wrists. They knew it was going to be a difficult case that would challenge their knowledge and expertise. As I lay there, feeling the pain and the fogginess of all the pain medications, I tried to stay calm and surrender into the pain. Over the next several days, I did my best to use the skills I had learned in yoga and meditation to surrender and find peace and comfort in the unknown, but it was such a struggle.

My leadership skills were called into action during one of the darkest times of my entire life. I wasn't sure if I would ever use my arms, hands and fingers again. Thoughts ran wild through my mind, and I wondered if I would recover. Had I made a mistake? Would I ever return to some level of normalcy? These questions dominated my thoughts.

When my recovery began, I felt emotionally empty, somewhat depressed, and not able to envision a path forward. I was relying on pain medication and simple moments of inspiration to get me through each day. After multiple surgeries, my journey continued with extensive physical therapy — exercises for both my arms, hands and fingers. This intensive therapy routinely required four to six hours per day. The nerves in my hand were contracted and scar tissue began to build. This limitation of movement prevented my fingers from opening and my wrist started to curve to a downward position.

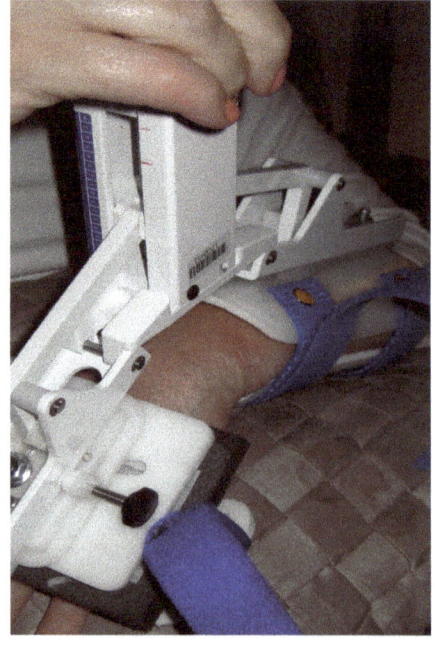

After months of physical therapy, I was given a special medical device to use for several hours each day, hoping it might improve my condition. After spending a tremendous amount of time and dedication, day after day using this device, the nerves and tendons finally released, moving beyond the scar tissue and allowing my hand to relax and open fully. I was finally experiencing success and the outcome of my leadership perseverance guided me toward a feeling of gratitude, self-compassion and an unwavering spirit for life.

I realize that each person has difficulties, traumas and sometimes life-threatening illness they endure and overcome, but what I discovered during my recovery is the power of self-leadership and its ability to determine if I would achieve success or stay stuck in the chaos of the unknown.

It is the game changer that determines if you experience healing and full recovery or continue to struggle to find your way forward. It is the energy and spirit of your desire to achieve success in each moment that determines if you will move beyond the challenge or continue to live in its shadows.

Each moment of my recovery, I had to generate inspiration for myself that sparked a strong will to recover, one that encouraged me to spend numerous hours every day doing extensive physical therapy exercises. During this time, I thought about the individuals who fail to see the light at the end of the tunnel and give up or give in to situations. Without the spirit of self-leadership, what appears to be a short-term challenge ends up being a long-term impact. Your ability to practice self-leadership and lead yourself forward during a challenging situation or during times of increased opportunities is essential to your overall experience of success.

After living with enormous feelings of uncertainty, I was finally feeling success. This was an experience that wouldn't have been possible without my unwavering drive to heal by committing to extensive therapy each day for months at a time. My inner strength and determination were finally reflecting the recovery that I desired. This two-year journey to recovery tested my spirit and took me to a place that I had never been before. An experience that left me feeling very grateful to be alive and ready to embrace the bold and empowered leader I knew I had become.

4. Learning to "Lean In" – A True Test of Leadership

My test of self-leadership strengths grew to a new level the day I discovered my legal team was having great difficulty getting the insurance companies to pay for my extensive medical claims. This delay in payment was being litigated due to a technicality of being injured in a work-related vehicle.

This new challenge took me down to a new low and tested every fiber of my being. Several months turned into two years, which felt like a lifetime. As I waited and wondered about the outcome of the legal results, I was left feeling empty — physically, mentally, emotionally and spiritually exhausted. My husband and I shared many moments of deep anxiety wondering how this could have ever happened. During one of these moments driving back from the court hearing, I felt an unfamiliar sense of inner peace come over me and I heard this little voice within me that said, *"Lean in!"*

All I could envision was a big, strong football player pushing a heavy piece of training equipment that weighs hundreds of pounds all the way down the football field. I heard the voice again. *"Lean in!"* I continued to listen and search for the meaning of what "lean in" meant to me. I shared this idea with my husband hoping the message of "lean in" might somehow console him.

Soon I realized this advice was about not giving up. I was being encouraged to put my head down and lean in to the pain, just like football players lean in to large pieces of training equipment to move them forward during practice. The spirit of leadership had once again risen within me, calling me forward to *"rise and shine."*

With this new level of awareness, I was ready to allow the pain to move through me without resistance, knowing it was my only path forward. I was able to let go of all the physical and emotional struggles and return to a state of inner peace — somewhere beyond this unbelievable experience. I knew my power resided in each choice and that I couldn't throw the pass off to the side or over the heads of the other football players, like some football plays dictate. I had to run the ball straight through the crowded middle, where I might be tackled, where all the other problems resided. I knew that my eventual success would be determined by how I responded to each moment. I could choose to react with fear, anger, frustration or I could respond with a compassion, hope, and knowingness that my situation would improve.

This was the turning point to my recovery. I released the emotional baggage that created an enormous weight on my physical, mental, emotional and spiritual health. It was a decision to embrace each moment with gratitude and release the anxiety of the unknown. Instead of living in fear, I chose to live from the perspective of knowing my life would improve.

Reflecting on my journey, I saw patterns and themes of leadership weaving through the course of my life. These accumulated experiences became the cornerstone of my inner strength and the primary principles for my work with others.

Exploring Mastery with the Masters

Over the next ten years after recovering from that accident, I tirelessly studied the principles of leadership from every master I could find. I became focused and fearless in my determination to experience a leadership presence that embodied a sense of ease, comfort and resounding impact. I was deeply committed to attending workshops and advanced retreats, working with well-known coaches around the world and truly dialing in to find the most advanced principles of becoming the best self-leader I could be. I knew that I had discovered a core element to life's success during my recovery, which would forever change the way I viewed leadership success.

After this extensive journey of deep discovery and reflection, studying meditation, yoga, the principles of Zen, Asian philosophies, Japanese art, neuroscience, and leadership wisdom from the greatest philosophers around the world, I realized my work was now being integrated into my life's work of art. The extensive hours of learning the principles of energy, quantum physics, leadership development, holistic wellness and design were all showing up and uncovering a new line of work as a Leadership Success Coach, Consultant and Workshop Facilitator. Through the many lessons of my journey, I now have the honor of working with individuals around the world to help them become strong self-leaders and self-masters of their work lives. I help them uncover barriers to great success and create their life's work as their masterpiece.

In my work, I now enjoy observing my clients experience true sustaining success inside and outside the workplace. I have the honor of watching accomplished professionals discover the many layers to their souls' desires, and step into a presence filled with joy, fulfillment and a sense of freedom.

LEADERSHIP IS A MINDSET AND PROCESS THAT INSPIRES ACTION

The true power and potential of leadership isn't about hoping something will change. It's about getting to the essential elements of our routines, behavior patterns and psychological conditioning to make meaningful lifelong changes. It's about the realization that attitude is a form of energy that has the potential to either build success or block success. In our time together, we will explore the concepts and techniques for shifting energy and how to generate, connect and maximize energy to create greater fulfillment and increased success. Together, we will open the door to unlimited success that is available inside and outside the workday experience.

If you're still with me at this point of the journey, I believe you, too, are ready and eager for workplace success. You are ready to redefine a new state of leadership that creates success from the internal place of freedom, fulfillment and flow combined with external success that is made of impact, effectiveness and measurable momentum.

The following chapters explore aspects of self-leadership, self-management and self-mastery, which are the three primary elements to becoming the Inspired Authentic Leader.

5. Breaking the Traditional Leadership Success Code to Become Unstoppable

We are on a journey together, working our way toward self-mastery and becoming the Inspired Authentic Leader of success inside and outside the work day. We will focus our partnership with boldness and curiosity as both are necessary allies to our journey ahead. Our goal to explore leadership and ensure deeper levels of measurable and sustainable success will be broken down into three key sections that offer both moments of inspiration, in-depth awareness and opportunities for self-inquiry and exploration. These sections include self-leadership, self-management and self-mastery, which are the three primary elements to becoming the Inspired Authentic Leader.

As we uncover valuable nuggets that each element offers, our focus will be on workplace success and experiencing inspired authentic leadership inside and outside the work day.

Previously we talked about our own definitions of leadership and the meaning it provides to our roles as leaders. To expand awareness and build a deeper connection to our leadership roles, it is important to increase our connection and explore the true meaning of **"being authentic"** as a primary leadership skill. How would you define the word authentic? What meaning does it have for you?

Authentic, for me, includes being genuine, with a natural flow of truth, inner peace and confidence in your ability to create and experience success. Being authentic instills a congruence in who you believe you are, with an expression that reflects the most natural qualities of your core being. Some of these desired qualities may include feeling centered, calm, confident and at peace with your experiences and surroundings. As you start to embrace your authenticity and increased confidence in your ability to succeed, you realize that regardless of the journey ahead, you have the knowledge and skills necessary to ensure your survival and success.

When you are "being authentic" there is a peaceful flow and congruence between who you believe you are and how you respond to each new experience.

How does that resonate with you?

In the pages that follow, my emphasis will be on the three primary elements to leadership success, just like pit stops at the three major cities along our trip together. The concepts, theories, ideas and inspiration listed will reflect a leadership position within the role of the working professional. However, each technique can be utilized as a success tool for any leadership role, both personally and professionally, to promote measurable and sustainable success.

Each of the three areas of leadership success builds upon the previous one. So, it's important to read through each section before moving to the next one.

The first element of leadership success is the section named Self-Leadership. This element of leadership is focused upon *"generating energy"* to create increased levels of fulfillment and optimized success. We will discuss self-discovery and our ability to call forth the leadership values that are aligned with the authentic self.

This is an opportunity to become more self-aware, to self-define and self-direct our leadership presence toward an ideal vision of success.

This section introduces the seven states of leadership success model that supports leaders in the ability to harness and lead their energy, so it works for them — not against them — to ensure success.

The second element of leadership success is named Self-Management. This section is all about *"managing your energy"* so it works for you instead of against you. We will establish a leadership presence that is aligned with increased awareness about "who you are being" and explore several thought-provoking questions, such as:

- Who are you at your core leadership presence?
- What combination of energy do you use to create success?
- What are the primary factors and areas of impact that either contribute or prevent you from experiencing success?

The self-management section is a bridge between the self-leadership and self-mastery success states. Self-management functions as a primary process, and it is the gateway to experiencing increased potential.

The third element of leadership success is called Self-Mastery. This section is focused on *"maximizing success."* It is designed to connect you to a personal connection for being the Inspired Authentic Leader and showcasing your own unique potential. It is the home for your personal discovery and a journey into experiencing the ideal leadership state of being. The purpose is to attain the experience and gain clarity associated with each feeling of joy, wisdom, freedom, flow, ease, passion, creativity and other emotions that are evoked by your experiences. This section is filled with a sense of coming home to the leadership presence you've always wanted to become. It is a unique place that holds the space for your leadership desires to unfold, evolve and be expressed.

Each leadership element is filled with rich wisdom and increased opportunities to combine awareness with expression, new insights into inspired action. Fear and frustration are transformed into freedom and flow.

At the end of these three sections you will explore the feelings of being exceptional, an experience that is deeply connected with the leadership presence of the Inspired Authentic Leader. This experience is filled with a vision of greatness and self-mastery skills that can be expressed in each of your leadership roles. During our time together, you will uncover your own unique experience of self-mastery and ultimately choose if you will decide to step up and into this new vision of success. Or to continue your journey on the path of traditional leadership success.

Regardless of how your journey unfolds, you will be in a new place of increased awareness, a place that is expanded and alive with the tools for greatness that each leader needs to become exceptional.

No journey is complete without a road map of awareness to depict each stop of our adventure and the highlights along the way. The road map provided on the next page starts with our intention to explore the potential of the Inspired Authentic Leader, with three primary stops along the way to self-leadership, self-management and self-mastery. You will learn to create your unique success formula that I call the **Leader's Edge.** This process will blend your experience into a sustainable success-producing formula for increased levels of success.

Your Pathway to Self-Mastery and Workplace Success

Are you ready?

Our journey together begins in the next section of this book with the experience of self-leadership.

Section Two...

Self-Leadership

6. Embracing Self-Leadership

Deepening our understanding of this key principle in self-mastery, we revisit the quote by Chinese philosopher Lao Tzu, "Mastering others is strength, mastering yourself is true power." It reminds us of the path to true power. Lao Tzu imparts timeless wisdom and great inspiration with this key point for our work together in this self-leadership section. This quote captures the true essence of our journey together as we direct our focus on the key elements of leadership. We begin the journey with self-leadership followed by self-management and then self-mastery, an experience of true power that reveals itself along the way.

Pause for a moment and reflect upon the potential of the quotation's meaning. What does it say to you? Does it impact you or offer insight of any kind? I hope it will resonate and connect with a deeper part of you, shining a light on a core aspect of your presence that is waiting and wanting to unfold. We all desire to make an impact, to contribute in a greater way, to feel heard, seen and valued for the contributions and insights we offer.

Self-leadership is the gateway to influencing others and leading them forward. Before we aspire to impact others we must first reflect, explore and rediscover who we are as individuals. It is necessary to increase our own awareness on who we are at the core of our values and the way we present ourselves to the world. Our goal is to establish a strong foundation of awareness, insight and new perspectives so that we can make a greater contribution, more impact and experiences of increased levels of authentic success. This is where self-leadership comes into play and opens the door to personal and professional greatness.

Self-leadership is our ability to inspire, motivate and lead ourselves forward to evoke the decisions and take action toward fulfilling our goals and desires. It is a state of self-awareness, self-definition and self-direction that puts you in a place of personal power. When you lead from a place of being in a robotic, automated type role, you are just a passenger. Self-leadership makes you the driver of your own success.

Self-leadership is about energizing yourself as a leader. It's not necessarily about doing more, it's about optimizing the success potential you already have.

Our ability to become strong self-leaders often starts in our childhood when we are given situations that encourage us to excel in some way or even to survive. As children, we have limited awareness and resources needed to respond to any given situation. Somehow in many instances, we experience an inner knowingness of pure awareness that shows us naturally the way forward. As an example, the following story conveys my first experience with self-leadership at the early age of nine.

The family crisis began on the day I arrived home from a school trip visiting Washington D.C. I ran through the door with the souvenirs that I couldn't wait to give to my parents and sister only to find that something was terribly wrong. As I entered the room the feeling was heavy, the expressions saddened, and I felt my laughter and excitement turn into fear. I felt completely overwhelmed with sadness, when I discovered my dad might not survive the unexpected surgery he was facing. He had been diagnosed with a malignant brain tumor that required surgery and extensive treatment.

On that day, a little girl with eyes filled with wonder and enthusiasm that lightened the room, became a leader. She became a leader who, over the course of the next several years, watched her dad struggle with surgery, extended hospital visits and cancer treatments that seemed never-ending.

My father was fighting for his life. I grew up living in the protection of a small country setting, accustomed to the love and security that both of my parents had always provided. With the unexpected news of my father's illness, I was now feeling alone, confused and unclear about what might happen next. In the midst of this experience, I remember feeling a strong inner strength and sense of determination to somehow make things better, to do my part as a contributor and offer support in any way I knew how.

My parents were both very strong individuals, but this new experience had shaken them to their core. A young child, I felt unsure of my role and how to handle the uncertainty that the situation created. My sister was equally overwhelmed with the magnitude of the uncertainty that stood before us. Her support was limited as she had recently married and was transitioning to her new role as a wife.

As I grew older, I began to increase my role and responsibilities from cleaning the house, doing the yard work, managing our family garden, taking care of myself and being the family cheerleader for inspiration. I was determined not to be an additional burden for my parents and, more importantly, I wanted to ensure that my family experienced moments of laughter and inspiration, so I stayed committed to focusing on the positive. I came up with daily rituals that made our time together enjoyable, even though we never knew from one minute to the next if each experience together might be our last.

As I recall this experience, I remember feeling a deep sense of knowing, inner strength and clear focus on what to do and how to do it. This inner strength that I now call "self-leadership" has been at the forefront of my natural skills and has continued to evolve over the course of my life. Although I had no idea of the energy that was transforming me at such a young age, I now realize this was the essence of the spirit for self-leadership that determines if we sit idle or take action, if we build success or block success.

When we are younger, we have limited awareness and experience on which to base decisions. However, underneath this lack of experience lies an innocence and pure knowingness from which to act. This awareness offers support for a state of self-leadership that is not questioned nor overpowered by our mental programming and learned tendencies.

As we grow into adulthood, our ability to become strong self-leaders is frequently impacted by the programming of past and routine behavior patterns we have developed along the way. The ingrained beliefs, mental chatter and self-talk are all influencers that take place in the background of our subconscious. We often lose our way from the natural flow of authentic forms of self-leadership as a young adult and transition into experiencing the limited perspectives of traditional leadership. Often, this is leadership that is thought-based, structured, well-defined and, often, void of intuitive awareness, possibility, creativity and inspiration that promotes the self-fulfillment we truly desire.

This journey that illustrates our transition from fear and a limited perspective to inspired action and limitless potential is the necessary path we all acknowledge and experience when becoming the Inspired Authentic Leader. This quest for self-leadership that takes you on the path to self-mastery reveals similarities to Joseph Campbell's book, The Hero's Journey, in which the hero finds true sustaining, fulfilling success.

Exploring Self-Leadership

**Self-awareness doesn't stop you
from making mistakes,
it allows you to learn from them.**

Let's continue to explore the true depths of self-leadership and our adventure into a state of self-mastery defined as the Inspired Authentic Leader. Our goal is to uncover the leadership presence and ultimate success you desire. Our focus will be upon three key aspects of self-leadership that include our ability to become self-aware, self-defined and self-directed. These three aspects of self-leadership will be broken down into sections which take you on a journey to exploring your own leadership presence and desired vision of success.

Self-Aware | Self-Defined | Self-Directed

Self-Awareness

Leaders who have taken time to explore their own inner leadership skills have discovered they have more success-oriented energy, or a success-advantage, that leads them to maximizing their success. Some benefits of becoming more self-aware include:

- A shift into a place of power, from the passenger seat to the driver's seat
- Acting and creating your desired outcome versus perceiving experiences as challenges and waiting for the challenges to change
- Increased health and overall well-being
- Greater feelings of connection, contribution, and creativity
- You show up and stand out with purpose and presence
- You get seen, heard and deeply valued

Self-leadership uncovers your ideal vision of success and pinpoints a leadership presence positioned to maximize your potential to excel.

Leadership is about choices and decisions that focus energy toward a specific desire or outcome. Your leadership strengths, weaknesses and roles play out each moment of your work day. They determine your ability to leave at the end of your work day either feeling fulfilled and impactful or ending the work day feeling unhappy and unfulfilled.

Your ability to choose and decide determines success. Step back for a moment to consider the influence and impact leadership has played on your career and work life success.

Let's break this down. As a young adult you most likely identified the field of study in which you wanted to build your skills. You selected the college or specialty school in which to gain the skill set, and once completed, put together an outstanding resume to attract your ideal job. During the job search process, you identified which jobs were most attractive, the interviews you hoped to win, the clothes you would wear, how you would respond to the interviewer's questions and ultimately, if given the opportunity, to choose which employment offer to accept. The quality of your leadership and the way you lead is the primary factor that determines your experience and the outcome you encounter.

Your level of success, fulfillment and other desired results all depend upon your ability to choose, decide and lead yourself toward success. The example mentioned above breaks down how leadership impacts your desired career potential. When we think of leadership, it's easy to forget that each choice and decision we make reflects upon our ability to lead.

In today's workplace there is no well-defined process to identify the best leaders who will ensure the highest level of success. Leaders are often identified based on credentials, performance, time in service and many other factors. However, if we explore the potential and many benefits that self-leadership has to offer, it promotes the question:

What if every employer, managing a small or large company, used self-leadership and the goal of self-mastery as their emphasis for creating success?

It is important to focus both on employee success and corporate success. Could this awareness promote increased levels of employee engagement, fulfillment, retention and productivity? Could it provide combined team, project, and corporate success that equates to people experiencing increased levels of purpose, passion, potential and profits?

I believe the answer is: **Yes!** That answer is based on my experience working across teams, projects, and Fortune 100 companies combined with stepping outside the corporate environment to become an entrepreneur and small business provider. Self-leadership and the desire for self-mastery is the game changer. It is a new perspective on what it means to win and experience increased performance, personal fulfillment and optimal success.

Embracing A New Perspective of Leadership Success

Self-leadership is the core element of success that pinpoints our leadership effectiveness. What if we had access to skills, tools and awareness that harness the quality of energy we need to maximize our success? Let's explore.

The Quality of Your Leadership Depends on the Quality of Your Energy

Yes, everything is energy. If we are serious about experiencing increased levels of success, then it's time to go to the core elements of our leadership potential to uncover the right strategies. At the subatomic level everyone and everything is energy. At the experiential level, I define energy as the dynamic movement that takes place to transition our experiences from one state to another state — from one experience to another experience, and from one leadership state into a new leadership state.

Albert Einstein proved this theory back in 1905 when he discovered that energy is in all things, the core substance from which all things are created. There are many descriptions to reference energy as a source state. Listed below are some descriptors of energy:

- Patterns of information
- The available power and capacity needed to perform
- Pure potential, strength, vitality and vigor
- Source of liveliness, an overall vibe, or spirit
- Source of enthusiasm, or spark

These descriptions are only a few ways to define the presence of energy and the impact it has on our daily interactions.

We all have our own way to describe energy, but do we ever stop to consider how it truly impacts our day-to-day success? For our work together, let's consider energy as the prime indicator of the quality of our leadership. As an example, our ability to create a leadership presence that reflects higher qualities of energy can optimize and maximize our work day experiences. Essentially, it is our responsibility to direct energy, so it works for us, not against us.

Our goal in this section is to pinpoint the key elements of self-leadership as it pertains to you, the individual. I will introduce you to seven states of leadership that will either build success or block you from experiencing success. As you work your way through the following chapters, I will invite you to take part in self-exploration and self-awareness exercises to pinpoint the key aspects of your ideal leadership presence.

Your Formula for Success Starts Here

To maximize your experience with the contents of this book, I recommend putting together a "leadership success playbook" as a home to each of your discoveries. I'll provide the tools, insights and exercises, and invite you to provide answers, ideas and a new awareness for creating a leadership success playbook that speaks to you. Select a binder in a color that feels appealing to you. This binder can have a professional feel or a whimsical, playful feel, you choose. Have fun; get creative. This is your own go-to "leadership success playbook," so be sure it reflects your sense of style. Create a cover for your playbook with a title that resonates, inspires and embraces your vision of success.

This playbook, regardless of the type you choose, will be the home for our work together. You create it to maximize success. As you work your way through each of the chapters of this book, you will uncover the awareness you need to experience both current and future success. I encourage you to set aside the time in a quiet place free of distraction to complete each exercise. Record and capture each of your ideas and ah-ha! moments of awareness. Once you've completed each of the exercises, print out the ones you feel make the most impact and place them in your "leadership success playbook."

Together, we will identify a leadership success formula that helps to create your ideal work experience and the success you desire. This awareness will continue to evolve, unfold and expand throughout the course of our time together and for years to come. My hope is that your "leadership success playbook" becomes a vital tool you will return to often as you identify increased awareness, insight and desires. It will function as a sustainable success-oriented tool for repeatable success for both short- and long-term goals.

In the next chapter, we explore an empowering tool –
the power of choice.

7.
The Power of Choice– Creating Your Vision of Success

One of the Primary Elements to Leadership is the Power of Choice. Each Moment Describes Who We Are and Gives Us the Opportunity to Decide If That's Truly Who We Want to Be…

In every moment of our work day, we are presented with numerous choices. Choices are vital to success, and the quality of each choice determines the quality of our work experiences. For example, do you show up to work each day with a sense of readiness, a feeling of renewed energy and inspiration, dressed to impress, ready to engage, and choosing to create success-generating work experiences? Or do you carry the leftover energy from the day before, feeling tired, uninterested and disengaged with a mindset of just getting through your work day? We have a vital choice to make as we begin each day to prepare for our work day. The choice is to create success or just surrender to daily demands. That choice can become imprinted in our minds, distracting us from reaching our desired goals and objectives.

Take a moment to recall your morning rituals and notice how you feel waking up and preparing for your work day. What feelings or sensations do you experience? Where do you feel the sensations in your body? What thoughts are going through your mind? Based on your thoughts, feelings and sensations, what actions do you take? What's the impact of your thoughts and feelings? Take notice of the automatic rituals that are being played in the background of your mind and influencing each morning's rituals to either invite success or block success. Notice the impact that each ritual has on your daily rhythm and overall momentum.

Capture any awareness that arises with the following exercise.

Preparing for Your Work-Day

Beliefs-Thoughts	Feelings-Sensations	Actions-Behaviors

What new insights do you have? Just notice.

How could this insight be affecting the quality of your experience and the quality of your success?

> *"Our futures are created from choices we make in every moment."*
> —Deepak Chopra

We are fortunate to have freedom to make choices. Between any stimulus or situation, a space exists. That space provides us with access to our greatest power, the power to choose. This power is the point of focus for creating strong self-leadership skills. A place of impact, influence and success-orienting energy that determines the quality of each outcome. This one powerful action determines our level of fulfillment, happiness, connection, contribution and all other high-quality experiences. It's the ability to choose how we will lead in every moment of our lives, inside and outside our work day.

The image below depicts the process of this response choice. First, a stimulus presents itself, followed by a pause of opportunity that exists prior to every response. This pause is your "power point" and the perfect opportunity to reflect on how you would like to respond. Once you have chosen your response, continue the process by communicating your decision to others.

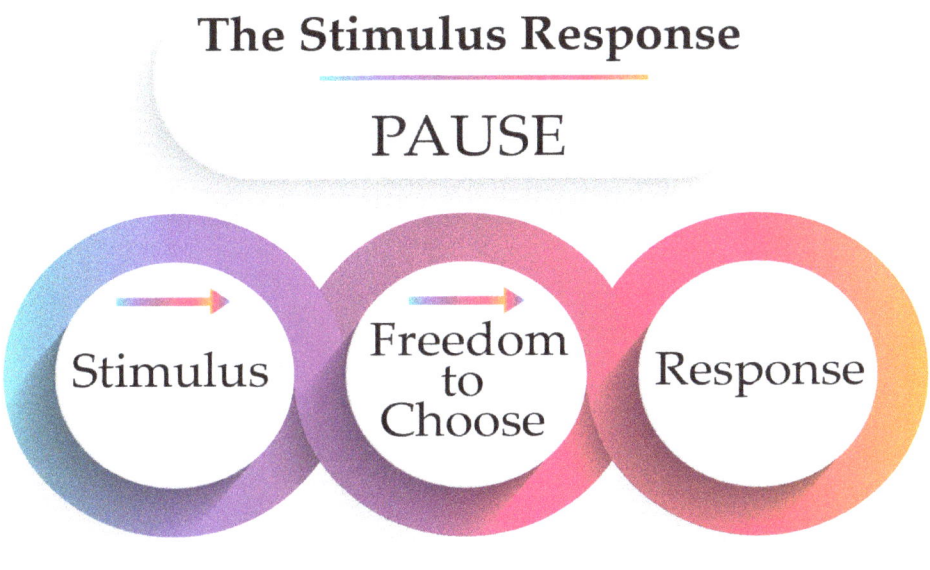

As we understand the importance of creating high-quality choices that are fueled by moments of assessment and reflection, consider using this process to determine which choice offers the most support to your success. Let's explore one primary choice that will be the cornerstone of our work together.

Self-Definition

What is the ideal vision of success for you? Consider this question any way you choose. You can focus on individual success, workplace success, project success, team success, leadership success and other successes that come to your mind. It doesn't matter how you structure this question. However, it is essential for you to identify a vision for what "success" looks like for you.

Another way to view this question is, "Where are we going in our work together?" As you reflected on the title and description of this book before reading it, something about it spoke to you. Something about the message ignited a pain or desire within you. What was that? Make sure you capture this clarity before moving on.

- Imagine your ideal vision of success is exactly the way you desire it to be.

- What thoughts are running through your mind?

- What are the emotions that emerge for you?

- Identify the qualities of your ideal experience.
  Where are you? What are you doing? Who is with you?
  Why are you doing what you're doing?
  How are you doing it?

- What new experiences will you have once you arrive at this new experience?

- What will have changed?

- What will you have more of, and less of, in this new experience?

- Just notice and capture your insights.

For our work together state your intention in one clear and concise sentence.

My Ideal Vision of Success is: _____

_____

_____

Together we will focus our energy toward creating your desired vision of success. We will align the quality of our focus, identify core choices, and give attention to key areas to ensure maximized success.

To kick-start the defining process, we will work through the three-step formula listed below to pinpoint the primary elements for creating a strong foundation that will function as the representation for your vision of success.

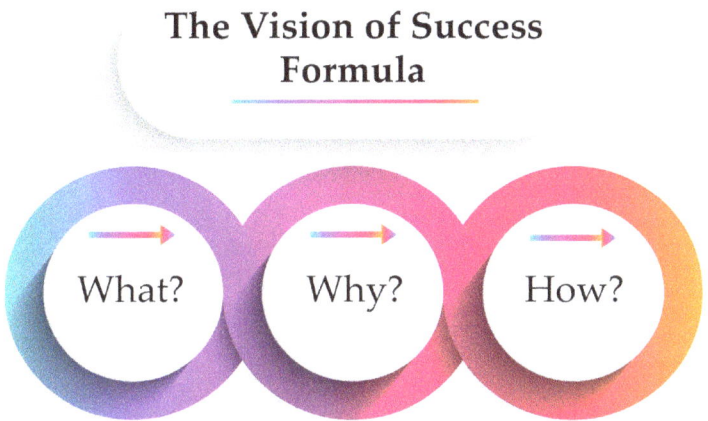

Creating Your Vision of Success

Defining an ideal vision of success is the "What" part of the equation. Now that we have identified the ideal leadership success vision and focused our energy, let's uncover the "why" factor to outline why your vision is important in the first place?

Why is this important to you? What's underneath the surface of the words that come to you when you ask this question? Just listen and notice what feelings and sensations show up in your awareness. Capture each insight as you ask: "why is this vision of success important?" Ask why and listen; once you receive an answer, ask yourself, "Why is it so important?" Keep drilling down and asking "why" until your responses repeat the same insight. Once you are comfortable that you have identified a clear "why" you want your vision of success, capture this description in a clear, concise way.

A sample statement: "I want to experience what it would feel like to lead from a place of total ease, comfort and great wisdom. To feel heard, seen, valued and empowered to make the impact I so truly want to make."

In the example listed above you will notice the "why" discovery identified several core values as being important and supportive to a potential vision for success.

What Motivates You to Excel?

This is a very important part of the inquiry so take time to capture all the insights that surface. Try not to judge. Just notice, capture and record.

Another layer of the "why" factor is in understanding what is motivating your desire for success? Is it a desire for a new car, a new position, new salary, greater fulfillment, more impact? Notice if the "why" factor is more tangible or intangible.

Create a list of motivators that drive your desire to experience success.

1.

2.

3.

Uncovering the Power of Values

Once you capture the new insight, consider exploring what values are most important. Values are the principles people live by, and the motivation that drives them. They are the ideas we have about what is good, bad and most important. When things are going well in life, your values are being honored. However, when things aren't going so well, one or more of your values are most likely being challenged.

During the period of birth to seven years of age, your values are imprinted into your subconscious mind as you monitor the impact of your actions on your environment and the influences of your parents, siblings, friends, family members and other people you encounter.

At approximately seven to fourteen years of age, you develop your values by modeling the values of others. As you continue to develop and mature into adulthood, you assess your values and prioritize them based on what's most important. Your values hold a significant power to cultivate your ability to experience success. You judge yourselves and others based on what you value.

Uncovering your primary values will help you understand which values are being challenged or missing from a situation and contributing to your dissatisfaction. Your ability to connect your values with the actions you take in life will determine your level of satisfaction and overall fulfillment of success.

There are two primary types of values: fear-based values and conscious-based values. The former develops values based on fear in order to avoid some consequence. Fear-based values lead to the sense that you "have to" do something instead of choosing to do something. Conscious-based values help people take positive action. They lead to actions you "want to" do, instead of to actions you "have to" do. Considering these parameters will help you pinpoint your empowering, conscious-based values that align with the qualities of your desired vision.

Identifying core values and applying them as a primary focus toward a desired experience produces success. If you are to experience deeper levels of fulfillment and increased success, you need to align your energetic focus toward the desired experiences instead of away from pain or some level of resistance. Too many times, you get caught up in an automatic ritual that keeps you feeling an increased level of resistance or avoidance. This may include the feelings of fear, frustration and similar emotions. By understanding your values and the impact they have, you become clear on which values are most important and which ones are less important.

Another way to consider the importance of values is to remember that values are *sources of energy with significant impact.* If you use your core values as a root or foundation on which to create and to act, this alignment of energetic potential is the success-oriented energy that optimizes your experience of success.

However, if you are not sure which values are most resonating to you, or you don't use your values as the primary source for decision making, it weakens your success potential, and the result is less than desirable.

Brainstorm a list of primary values that come to the forefront of your mind and capture them. View a complete list of values at: www.beyondstatusquo/values. Once you have several values listed, review and select the five top values.

My Top Five Primary Values Are:

1.

2.

3.

4.

5.

Values are the primary drivers to success. Values are the rocket fuel for why we resonate and take action toward some goals and the roadblocks that divert us from taking action on other goals. Identifying the "**why?**" that drives your desire for success is key.

Another helpful exercise in considering the "why" is asking yourself:

- **What do I want more of in my work life experience?**
  Example: (fulfillment, being heard, seen, valued, to be more effective)

- **What do I want less of in my work life experience?**
  Example: (competition, frustration, fear, status quo, boredom)

Continue to capture and record this information as we work our way through discovering the unique aspects of your self-leadership.

Deepening the "Why" Factor

Just as values are important to creating an authentic and purpose-filled experience, it is also necessary to determine your preferred beliefs, exploring the question, "What principles or beliefs will I use to lead myself and others toward creating successful outcomes?" These principles will become your personal foundation, one from which to lead others. Principles are life philosophies, a way of "being." They are the way to "walk the talk" and provide the opportunity to rely on your own beliefs throughout your daily experiences. These principles may include inspirational quotes, personal beliefs, mantras, poems or stories you use to feel inspired, engaged and driven.

As I mentioned earlier in my story, one of my unwavering beliefs is "failing is not an option." I do not envision experiences as failures; I believe all experience is feedback that can improve our next experience. The belief that "failing is not an option" keeps me inspired, energized and engaged with staying the course toward fulfilling my goals, instead of being distracted or losing momentum.

What Principles or Beliefs Will You Use to Lead?

You may notice that your responses might connect your values to your beliefs, which combine to create momentum. Create a list of your primary principles or beliefs. Example: There are no mistakes, only opportunities to learn and grow.

1.

2.

3.

4.

5.

As you delve deeper into your inner states of awareness and ask questions of discovery and reflection, it is essential to understand *why* something is powerfully important to you. Getting clear about the "what" is the vital first step. The next step is discovering the depth of the "why" to deepen your clarity and open increased potential. On the next page, record any insights related to why a value or belief is important to you.

1.

2.

3.

4.

5.

Example:
What?
I value balance. **Why** is balance important? I believe combining creativity and fun in my work day, while also experiencing increased levels of productivity, reflects the balance I yearn to experience.

In this statement, continue to ask "why?" for several intervals until you reach the insight that strongly resonates with you.

Example:
What?
I value morning meditation. **Why** is this belief important? I believe if I meditate each morning before starting my work day, I will feel more balanced. Why? Because when I meditate, I feel more peaceful and have more clarity, which contributes to better performance and increased fulfillment in my workday.

Defining the "why" factor is the crucial element to success and the fuel that propels your success forward. To deepen your awareness of the "why" that's driving your success, write each of your values and beliefs, adding why they are important to your success.

1.

2.

3.

4.

5.

Now that we have explored the two primary elements of "what" and "why" let's explore the "how" part of the equation.

How will you use your leadership skills to propel you forward to your desired experiences of success? How will you learn to focus the quality of your energy to align with your desires and make choices that lead to your vision for success?

Self-Direction:
Defining the "How" of Self-Leadership

The self-leadership work outlined in this book has been influenced by the clients I have served and supported as an Executive Leadership Success Coach, combined with the leadership positions I held throughout my extensive career. I continue to deepen my awareness and wish to acknowledge the beneficial impact of a leadership approach created in 1999 by Bruce D. Schneider, Founder of the Institute for Professional Excellence in Coaching. Bruce created a system called *Energy Leadership*™ based on a tool known as the *Energetic Self-Perception*™ chart.

Within the *Energetic Self-Perception*™ model, Bruce identified seven primary levels of energy that have various qualities, characteristics and associations of energy presented as core thoughts, feelings and actions. Using the inspiration from this concept of energy as a leadership quality will focus our work and guide us as we explore the "*how*" to develop a successful leadership presence. This concept of energy will be aligned with the primary thought, emotion and behavior patterns that determine the quality of our success. Each state will introduce the reader to a unique leadership perspective and state of leadership success. It helps leaders to experience who we are being as we choose each state to create our vision of success.

For example, each time you listen to a radio you tune in a specific frequency, a characteristic of energy that is being communicated to you. This energy is being transmitted through a frequency (or vibration) to create your experience. As you listen to the selected station, you may enjoy the experience and continue listening, or you might change the channel and experience a new genre. Each channel provides a new experience and offers the listener the power to choose how to use the radio's capacity. The seven states of leadership success offer leaders the power to choose which state they desire to experience and how they will use the characteristics of each state to create and maximize their success. In the next chapter, we define and begin to explore the seven states of leadership success.

8.
The Seven States of Leadership Success—
Leading Energy to Maximize Success

The Seven States of Leadership Success

Leadership is about leading energy and our ability to direct energy to create experiences that enhance our success and promote long-term, sustainable results. As we review the seven states of leadership success, I use the word "states" to encompass energy, qualities, characteristics and new insights. This word is an identifier for a grouping of primary thoughts, feelings and actions that align with each state of success.

The Two Types of Energy

There are two types of energy that determine success: anabolic energy that builds success and catabolic energy that blocks success. Anabolic energy is a generating, empowering, creative and supportive type of energy. It promotes a sense of inner peace, increased well-being and a feeling of ease. Catabolic energy is a destructive, resisting and constricting type of energy that evokes a feeling of increased pressure, with a sense of force and disruption that often produces stress related illnesses. Therefore, when working with the seven states of leadership success, it is important to consider which type of energy you're using to create success and which type of energy may impede your success.

Anabolic energy is healing energy that promotes increased well-being. It's a state of higher vibrational frequencies that resonates with homeostasis. It builds, restores, recharges and renews. Catabolic energy is focused on survival and an increased level of anxiety, which redirects healing resources to function in a state of problem solving and crisis management. When your health resources direct your focus to crisis resolution, you are no longer in a state of well-being.

Instead of being in a healing state, you are in a super-charged state, which depletes your energy and takes you out of balance — out of your homeostasis state. Catabolic energy breaks down your motivation, creativity and productivity.

The seven states of leadership success are shown in the chart on the next page; seven is the highest state and one is the lowest state. Leadership success state descriptors are listed, and each state's impact on success is shown. The outcome of each leadership success state and a seed word describes the energy of each state to enhance the understanding and potential experience of each state. With time and practice the information will unfold naturally.

The Seven States of Leadership Success

7 — The Mastery State
Impact on Success: **Builds Success**
Outcome: **Mastery**
Seed Word: **FLOW**

6 — The Creator State
Impact on Success: **Builds Success**
Outcome: **Greatness**
Seed Word: **UNITE**

5 — The Opportunist State
Impact on Success: **Builds Success**
Outcome: **Partnerships**
Seed Word: **POTENTIAL**

4 — The Cheerleader State
Impact on Success: **Builds Success**
Outcome: **Service & Support**
Seed Word: **BALANCE**

3 — The Status Quo State
Impact on Success: **Builds Success**
Outcome: **Awareness**
Seed Word: **SETTLING**

2 — The Dominance State
Impact on Success: **Blocks Success**
Outcome: **Control**
Seed Word: **FORCE**

1 — The Victim State
Impact on Success: **Blocks Success**
Outcome: **Struggle**
Seed Word: **RESISTANCE**

In my description of the leadership success states, I will clarify the unique qualities that live at each state of leadership success and detail the "collective states" and how they impact the outcome of your work day experiences.

State #1
The Victim State

The lowest state of leadership is the victim state, and the energy is catabolic. This energy is destructive and limiting, often prohibiting leaders from creating their desired vision of success. In this state, leadership is non-existent or limited in a person's ability to lead or move forward toward achieving goals. Some qualities of this state of leadership success include apathy, survival, guilt, self-doubt, fear, worry, judgment and embarrassment. It is a state of low self-esteem and self-worth blocked by conflicting beliefs about the past. Past conditioning prevents this state of awareness from taking inspired action toward creating a future of success. Awareness and opportunities are constricted at this level. As an example, imagine viewing a situation with narrow, tunnel vision or consider the view you might have if you're looking through a pinhole-sized perspective.

> **Leaders Associated with The Victim Leadership State of Success Might Experience:**
>
> **Primary Thoughts:** Victim type energy, "I can never win… I'm not good enough."
>
> **Primary Emotion:** Lack of interest, enthusiasm or concern, hopeless
>
> **Primary Action/Results:** Resistance, Lethargy, Limited to no forward movement

This is a true state of pure crisis and workplace survival. Although successful leaders will not live at this leadership state indefinitely, there may be instances when leaders briefly experience some or all qualities of this state. Before long, they will need to make a new, consciously aware decision to return to a state of leadership with more success-oriented potential. At this state, the goal is to help you identify situations in which this energy may be preventing you from experiencing the success-oriented energy you desire before taking your next steps.

Questions for Reflection:

- As I review this state of leadership, what comes up for me?

- When was the last time I experienced this state of leadership?

- What impact did it have on my workplace success?

- What action or impact will I capture to promote increased future success?

An example of this state of leadership is an individual in the workplace who appears to be unhappy and doesn't take actions toward improving the dissatisfaction they feel during their work day. They often feel a lack of control and react to situations instead of choosing a response aligned with their vision of success. They appear to be helpless, hopeless and look to others to lead them.

When individuals experience this victim state, they are not taking personal responsibility or practicing the principles and skills of self-leadership. They are most often living from a place of triggers and reactions instead of planned responses.

State #2
The Dominance State

In this state, leadership shows up in a command and control "dominant" state. This quality of leadership is still being experienced predominately in the workplace today. It is the primary contributor to increased stress, employee turnover, lack of employee fulfillment and decreased workplace success at the individual, team and corporate levels.

Some qualities of a dominance state of leadership include command, control, force, struggle, micro-managing, competition, judgment, arguing, demanding, supreme authority. The focus is on self-success regardless of the impact on others.

> **Leaders Associated with The Dominance Leadership Success State Might Experience:**
>
> **Primary Thoughts:** Winning is all about me, how can I get others to help me reach my goals? How can I increase my ability to win?
>
> **Primary Emotions:** Anger, resentment, competition, greed, blame
>
> **Primary Actions/Results:** Defiance, control, stress, disappointment, frustration, struggle, force, weak emotional intelligence

Although this is not a desirable state of leadership, it is more success-oriented than leading from state #1, the victim state. A leadership dominant state can be productive for a short time span but is not success oriented for extended periods of time. Leaders with this quality of leadership will eventually lose the respect of their team members. They will contribute to increased levels of stress and anxiety, and they will struggle with a lack of engagement and the productivity required to generate success.

Do you resonate with this level of awareness? Can you recall a recent situation when you experienced this energy in yourself or with others?

Questions for Reflection:

- As I review this state of leadership, what comes up for me?

- When was the last time I experienced this state of leadership?

- o What impact did it have on my workplace success?

- o What actions or impacts would I like to record?

State #3
■ The Status Quo Leadership State

This is a higher state of leadership and the first state of anabolic, success-building energy. It is energy that provides empowering, inspiring and productive qualities for achieving success. In this state, you may identify both emerging and seasoned leaders living at this state of leadership with a sense of momentum toward success.

In this state, the focus is most often on self-success instead of the success of others; however, it is success-oriented and can produce positive results. Some qualities associated with this state include settling for the status quo, rationalization, justification, tolerance and coping. There is an increase of emotional intelligence and self-responsibility that is necessary to generate success. As an example, this leadership state may present leaders settling for their current role or a situation limited in growth and/or promotion. The outcome of this state is limited experiences, justifying what comes up in life rather than being a leader who identifies opportunities to grow and excel toward a desired direction.

This is the first state of productive leadership when the leader realizes the self-responsibility of choice, and each decision is built on values and desired outcomes. Success lives at this state, but it is limited and does not reflect the increased potential that resides at higher states of leadership. The limiting factor functions as a safety-net experience. These leaders often remain in a safe and secure role, instead of stepping outside their comfort zone to explore new opportunities or to excel beyond their current state of success. There is limited growth, innovation, flexibility and creativity. Success at this state is predictable, and in most instances, it does not provide the deeper levels of fulfillment and optimized success desired.

Leaders Associated with The Status Quo Leadership Success State Might Experience:

Primary Thoughts: Focus winning toward self instead of the team. They often lead with the energy of: "I will win; if you win, too, that's okay." Their energy is directed toward self-motivation and self-fulfillment.

Primary Emotions: Relief, no conflict, security, stability, comfort

Primary Actions/Results: Limited success – keeps everything predictable without conflict

Individuals at this state are more empowered and aware; however, they continue to play a smaller game with the focus on keeping it simple, safe and inside the secure zone. You may discover these individuals inside the workplace living in positions with little to no flexibility, change or risk. They might stay in the same corporations or positions for an extended period to maximize their security, reducing the risk of stepping out into the unknown. These individuals can be a true asset to a company that desires stability in their employees to be reliable, predictable, and committed to keeping things in the status quo with little-to-no change.

Questions for Reflection:

- o As I review this state of leadership, what comes up for me?

- o When was the last time I experienced this state of leadership?

- o What impact did it have on my workplace success?

- o What action or impact would I like to focus on and record?

State #4
The Cheerleader State

This state of leadership is the glue of most organizations today and adds value to the reason individuals, teams and organizations succeed. Those who lead with the energy of the cheerleader state offer support and inspire others to excel and experience increased levels of success. These leaders are most often uplifting, team oriented, the leader in the center of the group who connects and ensures enthusiasm and engagement. They may enjoy helping others to feel good about themselves and inspire a team-oriented work environment. It can be a great leadership asset to inspire, motivate and influence others' success.

Some qualities associated with this state of leadership success include gratitude, love, caring, support, playfulness and inspiration. The challenge to this state of leadership is a layer of judgment based upon the assumption that other individuals may be helpless, needing the cheerleader's support for the individual being helped to excel. Conflict, confusion and frustration may occur when advice and leadership direction is given without the permission of the individuals receiving the support.

Leaders who lead from the cheerleader success state tend to focus solely on helping others excel and often lose sight of their own need to practice self-leadership. Sometimes, cheerleaders provide too much support to others and don't focus enough energy toward self-care and desired success. When the focus is out of balance and too much is directed to others, cheerleaders lose their success-oriented potential and lapse into the victim and dominance leadership states. When they are out of balance, they may notice feelings of stress, anger, worry, self-doubt, frustration, and similar experiences.
Leaders can experience tremendous success at the cheerleader state of leadership. Once they learn to balance their desire to impact others positively with practicing self-care and self-leadership for their own success goals, their leadership presence can be powerfully impactful and positive.

Leaders Associated with The Cheerleader State of Leadership Success Might Experience:

Primary Thoughts: You win, your success depends upon my support

Primary Emotions: Feelings of gratitude, love, compassion, service

Primary Actions/Results: Takes nothing personally, playfulness, dedicated emotional support to others

Questions for Reflection:

- As I review this state of leadership, what comes up for me?

- When was the last time I experienced this state of leadership?

- What impact did it have on my workplace success?

- What action or impact would I like to focus on and record?

State #5
The Opportunist State

Some of the greatest thought leaders in history lived, and continue to live, in this leadership state. It is a state of leadership that is based upon identifying opportunities, key partnerships and creating win-win successes. Those who lead from this state of leadership have transitioned from traditional forms of leadership into a new empowered and authentic leadership state. They are calm, confident and comfortable leading in uncertainty, viewing each situation as an opportunity to lead instead of a challenge to overcome. The focus is on creating a win-win for all individuals involved — whether the win-win is between two individuals or multiple groups of leaders and teams.

Imagine the impact of increased success for leaders across the board if they used the opportunist state of leadership as their primary leadership role. In this experience, leaders celebrate the impact of success across individuals, teams, groups, projects, clients and corporations served.

Some qualities associated with this state of leadership include fulfillment, confidence, authenticity, peace, acceptance and inner awareness, which are combined with the leader's outer performance as vital components for creating success.

Leaders who incorporate the "heart energy" associated with the cheerleader success state (# 4) with the "mind energy" associated with the opportunist success state (# 5) create and experience their own measurable success and the success of others.

Leaders Associated with The Opportunist State of Leadership Might Experience:

Primary Thoughts: Win-win situations, partnerships, increased opportunities

Primary Emotions: Calm, confident, authentic, centered

Primary Actions/Results: Fulfillment, profound impact, increased success

Questions for Reflection:

o As I review this state of leadership, what comes up for me?

o When was the last time I experienced this state of leadership?

o What impact did it have on my work place success?

o What action or impact would I like to focus on and record?

State #6
■ The Creator State

Masters who create art, music, poetry, beauty, design, and other creative genius expressions use the creator state of leadership to generate enormous amounts of joy, fulfillment, and increased success. This state of leadership is the home to intuition, deeper awareness, insight and expression. This leadership state empowers the leader to go beyond external awareness to incorporate an expanded awareness connected to a source of greatness outside themselves. Leaders at this state are deeply authentic, they are empowered with a vision for being exceptional. They have the tools and skills required to create immense success.

▎ **Some Qualities Associated with The Creator State of Leadership Success Include:**

Unity, non-judgment, synergy, openness, joy, great wisdom, a sense of oneness, and a whole-being perspective that views situations from their fullest potential. The energy of this state is highly creative, intuitive and empowering.

Leaders rarely remain in the creator state of leadership; however, with practice and awareness they can use the wisdom and creative power of this state of leadership to support their own innovation and create highly skilled teams of success. They can establish a vision for greatness that creates the unthinkable in leadership awareness.

Primary Thoughts: Unity – everyone wins, it promotes synergy and unifies everyone as one team, one success

Primary Emotions: Joy, fearlessness, oneness

Primary Actions/Results: Wisdom, access to intuition, a vision of greatness

Imagine the impact of employee satisfaction, performance and success if leaders in all roles included the creator state of leadership into their work day. Leaders as individuals would view their work experience as a work of art, their work life as an artistry that defines their impact and their work success as a masterpiece of core values and visions of greatness.

Having the ability to tap into this state of leadership is powerful and life altering. By increasing our awareness and connection with this creator state we can activate the power of this energy as needed to promote more creativity, inspiration and fearlessness for increased levels of success.

Questions for Reflection:

- o As I review this state of leadership, what comes up for me?

- o When was the last time I experienced this state of leadership?

- o What impact did it have on my work place success?

- o What action or impact would I like to focus on and record?

State #7
The Mastery State

The most powerful leaders in the world experience temporary access to this state of leadership. It is the state of pure potential. Although no one has full-time access to the mastery state of leadership, we can access it as we increase our awareness on the qualities that live within this experience.

This state is filled with absolute passion and potential where all possibilities exist. It is home to our deepest desires and visions. While in this state, leaders lead from a self-mastery state and have access to the other six states of leadership success to use as they desire. They have the unique ability to lead from each state depending upon the need or desire they experience to create their vision of success. Just like a master pianist uses all 88 keys on his piano to create a masterful composition of music, leaders with a self-mastery presence have the flexibility to use each of the seven states of leadership success to create their desired experience of success. In one situation they might embrace the opportunist, creator or mastery states of leadership to ensure maximal benefits of success, while at other times they may use the power of the status quo and cheerleader states to interact with coworkers who may relate to the energy of those leadership states.

When leaders lead from the self-mastery state, it may be difficult for other individuals to connect, understand, or relate to their leadership presence. Therefore, those who lead from the mastery state must be able to tap into all other states of leadership to connect, contribute and create success based on the energy required to incorporate the desired outcome.

Qualities Associated with The Mastery State of Leadership Success Include:

A feeling of abundance, freedom, purpose, passion and increased potential. Non-judgment is a key aspect to this level of leadership. Leaders lead from a place of acceptance of all experiences, all levels of success. They understand the importance of the journey and release all attachment to the outcome. They embrace the power of now to experience the beauty of each moment, one experience at a time.

Imagine how this level of leadership might impact employee engagement and employee workplace satisfaction, promoting full engagement in each day's work experience. If we are open to embrace each moment, free of any attachments to a defined outcome, how would this increase the fulfillment of each experience?

What if we had the ability to liberate ourselves from fear and frustration and lead from a place of true success where all potential lives? The moment we release expectations on how our work experiences should appear, we release judgment and embrace a true mastery state. We free ourselves to enjoy the journey of our work day and remain open to embrace the potential of each moment. The mastery state is the greatest potential that exists for leadership, it is a leadership presence that is filled with unconditional love and unlimited success.

> **Primary Thoughts:** Non-judgment, winning and losing are illusions, the focus is on each experience as it unfolds naturally, effortlessly.
>
> **Primary Emotions:** Absolute passion, freedom, flow and fulfillment
>
> **Primary Actions/Results:** Pure creation, having the ability to create your desired success free of struggle. This is a state of ease.

In comparison, we mentioned in the victim state of leadership (#1) that individuals who used the victim leadership success state experience a limited and narrow view of perspectives. The opposite is true in the creator and mastery leadership success states. Opportunities and perspectives continue to expand at higher states of leadership success. Instead of viewing a situation from a narrow perspective, the viewpoint is expanded into a limitless range of potential.

We have now previewed each of the seven states of leadership success, I invite you to reflect on the qualities of each state and explore the impact that each experience provides. All seven states offer leaders the ability to use each state as a reference framework for experiencing a leadership presence with enormous success. This framework is a valuable tool to use individually and collectively, as it provides a point of reference that everyone can use to create success. It provides a standard mode of communication by calling out each state as a unique quality of leadership success.

Leadership in Action

Having a frame of reference creates a strong foundation, but how will you apply the knowledge gained? The first place to start is to identify experiences within your work day that reflect each state of leadership success and notice if the state is a success-building or success-blocking experience. Does it give you a sense of creativity, inspiration, and expansiveness or are you working in the victim or dominance state – with limitations, challenges and an experience of diminished success?

The seven leadership success states offer a support tool with endless possibilities and potential. Just like a flower bud opening gradually to a full bloom, your reflection on the seven leadership success states will unfold naturally and lead you to new experiences of unlimited success.

Status Quo or Beyond Status Quo?
Are You Limited or Limitless?

Another way to use this reference model is to ask yourself: are you leading with the limited qualities of the status quo leadership state (# 3) or the qualities of a more productive, success-oriented opportunist state (# 5) or the creator state (# 6) or (# 7) the mastery state?

The seven states of leadership success each offer value at different times in the work day. Our leadership goal is to expand our awareness of each state and practice dynamic leadership. When we practice the art of being dynamic and learn to identify the state of leadership that is needed in the moment, we take on a powerful state of leadership success. We better communicate our needs to others, connect more deeply with individuals who reside in different states of leadership and begin to create, experience and express our connection to increased success.

Let's consider a few examples of how each of these states may show up in the workplace.

To define the examples of each state, I will use a character reference by the name of Janet. She is a seasoned career professional, age 47, who has experienced significant success in her life. However, Janet feels she is no longer fulfilled and wants to identify a leadership style that is more authentic and more emotionally rewarding. She yearns to experience opportunities to express her values of contribution and impact.

How will Janet's leadership presence show up in each state?

THE WORKPLACE SCENARIO

Janet recently submitted her resume for a new position as Director of Engineering. She has an extensive history of enormous success in the technology field and believes she is well qualified for the new position. When she submitted her resume, she had high hopes of being selected as the candidate to fill the role. Several days after her interview, she learned she had not made the list of final candidates being considered for the open position.

How will each state and quality of leadership determine her experience and response to this situation?

#1 The Victim State: *Leadership Struggle*

Once Janet learned she was not selected to fill the position, she felt rejected and not good enough. She wondered what qualifications were lacking from her resume that did not warrant her the job. Now she is worrying and feels fearful about not being selected for the open position, wondering if this is an indicator of her value to the organization. She questions her age, her skills and her leadership style — seeking evidence of lack. She is leading from the victim state of leadership and feeling she is not good enough.

#2 The Dominance State: *"Fighter" Leadership Dominance*

Once Janet discovered the interviewing panel was not going to invite her to a second interview for the position, she became angry and asked around to identify the names of the final candidates. After learning each candidate's name, she immediately assessed and compared their skills to hers, picking apart their credentials. Her anger escalated and she was determined to let the interview panel know their process was unfair. She blamed the timing of her interview being held late in the afternoon for not being selected as a final candidate. Her leadership presence, the dominance state, is one of denial, non-acceptance, and looking for a way to blame the outcome on others.

#3 The Status Quo State: *Leadership Awareness*

Once Janet knew the interviewing panel did not select her into the final interview process, she rationalized the interviewing process. "Yes, I knew it was a long shot, since there was a large team of participants," she told herself. Then she remembered a time in the past when she submitted her resume for a position and was not selected as the final candidate. Now she feels the outcome is predictable and she understands that sometimes things just don't turn out the way you'd hoped. She tells others she was not the applicant selected and that she wants nothing but the best for the new candidates being invited for the second interview. Janet is in a rationalizing state, using the energy and attitude of the status quo state. She reconciles this experience through her belief that "good is good enough."

#4 The Cheerleader State: *Leadership of Service and Support*

As Janet discovered the interviewing panel had not selected her to take part in the final interviews, she shared her tips and insights with the candidates selected on how they might win the position. She extended herself as an active advocate of service and support in helping other participants increase their chances of being selected. In time, she had forgotten to acknowledge the pain and sadness she experienced. Janet's leadership state was primarily one of service and support to others. However, in time she feels out of balance and notices she was caring so much about others, that she forgot to nurture her own needs and emotions.

#5 The Opportunist State: *Leadership Partnerships*

Janet discovered that the interviewing panel had not selected her to take part in the final interviews and immediately asked the names of the other candidates being considered. Once she discovered the candidate's names, she smiled, filled with joy. She knew the candidates and had enjoyed working with each one in previous roles. She immediately began to explore ideas on how she could create a win-win strategy in her ability to partner with each candidate for increased levels of combined success. She was elated with the interviewing process and excited to hear the results. Janet's focus was directed toward the opportunity, the excitement of the process, the candidate selected to fulfill the role and how she might add value to the candidate's success as well as her own. This focus on combined success, allowed Janet to experience a feeling of contribution and increased levels of success collectively as an individual, a partner and as a key contributor.

#6 The Creator State: *Leadership Greatness*

When Janet received the news that she had not been selected as a candidate for the final interviews, she laughed with joy. She recalled the enormous fun she had experienced during the interview process. She mentioned feeling a sense of creativity in her answers each time they asked her a thought-provoking question.

She stated that it put her in a place of discovery. As she asked the names of other candidates being considered, she used her intuitive skills to identify the collective potential of each candidate's strengths. She realized that each candidate's strengths were complimentary, and if combined, could provide greater impact to the position. She submitted a recommendation to the interviewing panel that outlined a solution for creating a mastermind team. Her suggestion pinpointed the combined skills of the core team and suggested using a unified approach instead of filling the company's needs with one primary candidate. The panel considered the recommendation brilliant and innovative and the outcome was enormous.

#7 **The Mastery State:** *Leadership Mastery*

Once Janet discovered that the interviewing panel did not select her to take part in the final interview process, she began to share her admiration for the beauty of the interview process. She mentioned her appreciation for the opportunity to share her skills and strengths with others. Her focus was on the process and how much creativity and fun she had experienced while being considered. She commented that it really didn't matter which person won; she knew each candidate would work seamlessly to fulfill the needs of the organization. Janet's ability to be in the moment, to bask in the beauty of the interview process and to envision all candidates working together to create success was remarkable.

This vision shows Janet's ability to lead from a mastery state, a leadership state filled with unconditional love for the process, the candidates involved and the combined success to follow.

We have uncovered each of the seven states of leadership success and observed our character, Janet, experiencing the awareness and impact each state has on her success. In the victim and dominance states, Janet experienced low levels of success, if any. In the status quo state, she was quick to settle and rationalize not being accepted as the final candidate. Since she wasn't selected previously, she felt there was a strong possibility she might not be accepted this time. Her attachment to past experiences impacted her energy for fully aligning with the new opportunity to grow and excel.

Only in the cheerleader state did Janet attract increased levels of success. However, her energy was all directed toward helping others achieve success, with limited focus on her own needs. She felt unfulfilled, frustrated and possibly experienced moments of the victim state. When she considered the opportunist state of leadership success, she experienced true success built on a win-win relationship between all parties involved — notable success that considers challenges and opportunities as potential to excel, instead of being show stoppers.

As Janet continued her journey to the creator state, she experienced the joy, wisdom and intuitive power of her leadership strengths to create synergy with all things, people, processes and potential. This was an opportunity for Janet to tap into her joy for creativity and deeper insight.

Finally, as Janet showed her ability to lead in the mastery state, she released any attachment to being selected as the candidate to fill the prestigious position she once desired. Instead, she noted the beauty of the interviewing process and her experience of being in the moment with the unconditional love she felt for all the people involved — and for their combined potential.

In the next chapter, we explore the wisdom inside challenges that often appear to be obstacles blocking the pathway to success.

9. Exploring the Rocks on the Pathway to Success

Discovering the Wisdom inside the Challenge

Rocks are rigid and appear to be obstacles on our path to self-mastery and our desire to experience increased levels of success. However, I developed a new perspective on the purpose of rocks while discovering paths to becoming the Inspired Authentic Leader. I now see rocks as a symbol of self-leadership and a necessary element to traveling on the road to our deepest desires.

As a child living in the rural areas of the country, I grew up discovering and playing with rocks as a form of creativity. I was captivated by their shapes, sizes, distinct colors and textures. Our family spent several weekends working on our land to clear pathways and remove rocks so we could access other pathways or create a desired setting.

Rocks have always been a fascination for me, but I never viewed rocks as "masters" on the journey to success.

Have you ever experienced a time in your life when you had a vision or desire that you were trying to achieve, and instead of experiencing a path of support and ease, you experienced a form of resistance at every turn? From my experience, this resistance has a similar quality and feel as a large, heavy rock blocking the path of moving in a desired direction. It's so disheartening to be headed down a path of self-discovery and experience a large bolder standing in your way.

This boulder that I'm referring to is often another person, some unexpected circumstance or it can present as many other forms of challenging experiences. These situations offer an element of shock and surprise when you are going in a direction that you believe is the right way. Then, suddenly, you're met with a form of resistance that stops you in your tracks. Does that mean it's not the right path for you?

Considering Janet, introduced in the previous section, this experience with an obstacle might include a person you respect and admire or with whom you feel a connection. Perhaps someone you believe could offer support to your success suddenly appears like a giant rock, blocking your path with a rigidity that halts your journey and leaves you confused. You realize this person is not the right person with whom to share your ideas or insights. This person is not the trusted partner you anticipated. Instead, this person is a rock placed in your path to slow or stop your progress by expressing doubts. "Hey, you're headed in the wrong direction!"

Consider that the obstacle could be a reminder that you don't need the guidance or approval of others, so you must find your own way. The rock's message may differ in various situations, but the sense of the resistance is clear. This rock is a firm reminder that something is not in alignment with your greatest experience of success. Although it is disheartening, mind boggling and deeply frustrating, if given the opportunity, it can provide access to your life's greatest answers.

Let me explain:

As a seasoned coach, I have spent a lifetime exploring questions like "Who am I?" "What is my purpose?" "How can I have the greatest impact?" "What does the expression of greatness look like for me?" In my early adult years, I often searched for mentors or other leaders, coaches with greater insight to enrich my awareness and offer support to my journey of increased awareness. I sought to understand life's most challenging questions, essentially to combine forces in thought and discovery. From my perspective, the greatest gifts shared are inspiration, accountability and support.

In my quest to explore wisdom, insight and deeper levels of awareness from others, some of the gifts came in the form of statements, such as:

- o "The answers are within you."

- o "Seek and you will find."

- o "Knock and the door will open."

These responses left me confused, frustrated and feeling like a large boulder had somehow landed in the path before me. When I first received the response "the answers are within you," I felt like I was trapped in a congested maze, challenged to resolve the puzzle and find my way home.

Do you relate to my experience? Have you ever experienced a person or situation that affected you like a large rock of resistance put in your way to hinder your progress?

In my discovery, these rocks take me back to a place of self-leadership that recognizes the value of rocks. Self-leadership has the expanded awareness to embrace the rocks and discover the messages they offer. I have encountered a lot of rocks, both physical rocks functioning as roadblocks in my journey and metaphoric rocks, who were influential people trying to divert me from the path I needed to take.

Although it's never pleasant to experience a rock of resistance, I now understand how to look for the value in the rock. The rock always has a message to offer. The message can be an indicator that the person you are talking with is not in alignment with your goals and desires. The rock may be alerting you that you're headed in the wrong direction and need to reconsider your strategy. A rock might simply serve as a reminder about the importance of practicing sound self-leadership skills — an opportunity to search within yourself and find your own way forward instead of looking to others for approval or support.

Once you understand the message of the rocks, or other forms of resistance, you will encounter fewer obstacles showing up in your life. You learn to embrace both the rocky and smooth paths, as both are equally important to transforming your life and leadership skills.

This awareness is often a tough lesson to comprehend, but for each metaphoric rock I have encountered, there is a way to transform the rough, hard experience into a smooth, inviting experience simply by shifting your perspective on the rock. Instead of viewing the rock as a point of resistance, transform your perspective so you can view the rock as a guiding factor for increased success.

In my case, I realized that if I was going to be a strong advocate for helping other leaders find their way to living and leading with increased experiences of success, I must learn to recognize and value the rocks along my pathway and be inspired to become a strong, solid rock of inspiration for others. I must reflect the qualities of self-mastery as one who is truly ready to hold a place of inspiration for other leaders. Like the rock, I need to stand firmly with a strong presence and function as a guide for others on the path to becoming an Inspired Authentic Leader.

What type of rock are you?
Are you a rock of resistance or a rock that offers support and inspiration for others when they are headed down a difficult path?

My perspective on rocks has transformed so deeply that I now view rocks as if they are all diamonds that have gone through intense pressure before being mined from the earth, cut, crafted and polished to perfection.

The next time you encounter the feeling of resistance, try labeling this experience as a metaphoric rock. Imagine a vision for the characteristic qualities of the rock and make it as vivid as possible. Does it feel rough, rigid, cool? Is the tone of the person speaking to you sharp or soothing? Do you feel your chest contracting or expanding?

Once you have a vivid description in mind, observe it from every angle and ask yourself, "What is this resistance trying to teach me?" "What is the opportunity here?" "Why is it blocking me from continuing in my current direction?" "What actions do I need to take instead?"

As you listen for messages about the feelings of resistance, identify an image of a rock that is strong, supportive and centered with the awareness of wisdom, insight and intuitive connection. Learn to transform rocks of resistance into rocks of support, beacons that keep you on the best path forward to experiencing your vision of success.

Regardless of whether you view resistance as a rock or some other inspiring image, each experience offers value, wisdom and insights that are vital to the timeliness of your fulfillment and success.

Bringing it All Together

We now have a solid foundation for self-leadership. We have identified the *What*, *Why*, and *How* factors that create the foundation for experiencing success.

- o We defined the *What* by identifying our ideal vision for success statement and the motivators driving that vision.

- o We defined the *Why* by pinpointing the primary values that captured why the factors, combined with beliefs, are important to us.

- o We defined the *How*, the final element of the three-step equation to creating success, by exploring the seven states of leadership success for creating movement and giving wings to the success we desire.

I have provided a lot of information in this chapter, and I commend you for sticking with the process!

Let's Recap Our Intentions

What: Recap your ideal vision-of-success statement and the motivating factor that is driving your vision forward.

Why: Recap the top five values that will fuel and give energy to your success statement and the principles and beliefs you will use to strengthen them.

How: Identify the vehicle that will transport your desired success into your daily experiences. Select which state of leadership success you will use to propel your vehicle forward. Your choice may be a combination of leadership states, including different qualities from each state.

The information provided up to this point may be new to you, and it will continue to expand as we work our way through the seven states of leadership success in this book. For now, identify your connection with each state, and pay close attention to the impacts that each state offers and how it either builds success or blocks success. Notice the energy of each state that supports, contributes to and boosts your success. Notice when the energy limits, resists or inhibits success. Just notice and allow yourself the time and patience needed for the new information to resonate and integrate with your current state of leadership awareness.

As you feel more comfortable with each of the seven states of leadership success, create an outline or strategy with as much detail as possible. This strategy may include thoughts that came up as you worked through one or more of the states, associations you made to current situations, insights on how to use a specific state to create more success or characteristics of a state that deter you from reaching the success you desire.

A defined strategy creates more energy, momentum, and potential for ensuring success.

Have fun with this exercise and don't forget to add your ideas, insights, and core strategies to your leadership success playbook we described previously.

Key Takeaways:

- o Experiencing workplace success requires a solid vision of your desired success.

- o Using the *What-Why-How* success formula provides the detail and defined movement you need to excel.

- o Success depends on your willingness to reflect, record and redefine your experiences with each state of leadership success.

Now that we have a better understanding of self-leadership, let's move forward to exploring how to put it all together in the self-management section.

Section Three...

Self-Management

10. What Type of Energy are You Using to Generate Success?

Self-Management is the process of uncovering the way you show up for life and how you identify influences that impact you and your actions.

Self-Management shines the light on each aspect of your attitude and behavior patterns to reveal your current leadership potential. The real question to consider is, are you creating increased experiences of success potential by tapping into higher states of leadership success or are you stuck in the limited leadership experience creating success from a limited space?

Self-Management opens the door to long-term sustainable success. It's rooted in the awareness of who you are being in each moment and your level of engagement for creating, expressing and experiencing your core attributes individually or collectively with others.

In this chapter, our work together is to assess which state of leadership you're using to create success compared to its impact. We will identify areas of optimization and transformation for increased success. Every situation we experience is an opportunity to create and experience success. The more we understand and use the energetic components that create success, the more power and potential we will have to transform our lives, leadership states and workplace experiences toward a state of self-mastery.

As we revisit our goals for becoming an Inspired Authentic Leader, a state of self-mastery, it is important to understand who we are as individuals. We need to understand how our perceptions of ourselves and others create and impact our world. Before we go in depth on this topic, let's explore how we perceive ourselves.

Inspired Discovery

Who Am I?
How would you describe yourself? Take a moment and brainstorm, without judgment, a few keywords you would use to describe yourself. Record both positive and negative descriptors that come to mind. Ask yourself, "Who am I?" Listen without judgment to the information that surfaces.

Example: I am driven, bold, fearful, creative, stressed. As you brainstorm this question, add color and expression to bring this exercise to life. Record as many words, thoughts, ideas and even visuals that come to mind. Consider drawing a little avatar or emoji that resembles this expression of yourself.

You can use the words "*I Am*" followed by adjectives or descriptors to uncover your core traits. The words "*I Am*" are powerful, potent creators; whatever you place after each of these words becomes more energized and active in a creative nature.

Once you have recorded 20 to 40 words that best describe you as an individual or as a leader, take notice of the ones that are success oriented and put a circle around them. Also take notice of the ones that might prevent you from experiencing success and place a square around those. Again, no need to judge. Notice and chart them accordingly.

Who Am I Being?
Next, take out an additional piece of paper and assess your current state of being. This question might be a little awkward at this point in our journey but ask and notice what comes to mind. Just listen without judgment to the information that surfaces. Where does

your emotional energy live? Do you feel excited, bored, focused, distracted? How about your spiritual energy? Do you feel you're on purpose by working through the information in this book or do you feel distracted? How do you feel physically? Relaxed, tense, in pain, constricted or expanding? Capture as much information as possible to describe your experience of feelings and sensations and record your observations.

What values are being expressed as you work through this exercise? Notice your physical presence and the way you convey yourself to the world. What type of clothes are you wearing? What colors are being reflected through your wardrobe, accessories, and other forms of expression? Are you dressed in subtle dark tones or are you wearing brighter tones? What message does this convey?

As you focus on your presence, note your expressions. Look in a mirror to record your facial expressions and think about the words you use to describe your current conditions. What tone of voice do you notice that describes the quality of words being used to express your intentions? Do you notice frustrations or fears underneath the surface you're not sharing with others?

Where are you directing your focus right here and now? Are you fully engaged in the moment or feeling distracted by other thoughts?

This awareness is information to record. As we work our way through each exercise, I will present new insights that continue to build on the awareness discovered here.

These questions define a self-image or visual experience of "who you believe you are" and depict a model of how you share and express yourself to others. As we continue to work with the seven states of leadership success, we will understand the concept of energy as the creative substance behind each thought, feeling, emotion and behavior pattern. We will build the connection between the energy we use to create success and the impact or outcome we experience from the energy being used in the creative process.

Creative Energy = Type of Energy + Quality of Energy

The Type of Energy = Leadership Success State. Which of the seven leadership success states does the energy express?

Quality of Energy = Primary energy used to generate Thoughts + Feelings + Actions + Results. This is the energy at the root of each expression.

Our focus in self-management is to uncover the game changers to success, to get clear on why we experience success in one situation and struggle in others. To understand what sits at the core of our behavior patterns that creates success and what keeps us from experiencing the success we truly desire. To ensure we reach a desired level of success, it is important to understand the creative process that takes place each time we select a combination of thoughts, feelings and actions. As we review our creative energy, the focus is on our attitude as "energy." That includes thoughts, feelings and actions that determine our results and overall success.

The Creation Formula

Your quality of success will depend upon the quality of the energy being used to drive success.

We all enter the world without an opinion or belief about anything. According to Dr. Bruce Lipton PhD, "from birth through the first six years of our life a child's brain records massive amounts of information on how the world works." By observing the behavioral patterns of people in their immediate environment — primarily parents, siblings, and relatives — children learn to distinguish acceptable and unacceptable social behaviors. The perceptions gained before the age of six become the fundamental subconscious programs that shape the character of an individual's life.

As an individual continues to grow, develop and learn while maturing into adulthood, the surrounding world influences the person's core beliefs, values and filters that determine success. As our beliefs and values become established, we function on "auto pilot," until we experience dissonance and question our beliefs. Even though there are many influences that impact our values and beliefs, we have the power to increase our awareness and test the degree to which each belief supports us or holds us back. As a result, we can make new choices and identify new empowering beliefs to replace the older, dis-empowering beliefs to increase our experience of success.

Your thoughts, feelings and actions can either set you up for success or hold you back.

Let's explore a few primary beliefs and consider their impact.

- If you believe you are powerful, creative and capable, you might feel confident and peaceful. As a result, you are more likely to take on challenges to grow and excel.

- If you believe you are below average, limited or vulnerable, you might worry or feel fearful. As a result, you may stay in your comfort zone and resist change of any kind.

To create success, you must recognize the thoughts and feelings that get in the way of experiencing success and explore their impact. The awareness of unsupportive thoughts can lead to challenging the perspectives that created them.

Each person has their own unique way of showing up in the world. This sense of self drives the way you express your thoughts, feelings, and emotions from the behavioral patterns you've established throughout life. Your behavior is the reoccurring way you respond to stimulation, including how you perceive each experience, how you assign meaning and importance to it, and how the experience ultimately determines your current conditioning.

Behavior Patterns Include:
Beliefs + Thoughts + Feelings + Actions = Outcomes or Results

Beliefs are the beginning of the creation process, the creative spark that sets the success creation in motion, and ultimately determines the experience of success associated with the outcome of your behavior patterns.

Your beliefs are the most fundamental critical factors to your success.

Beliefs are programmable into the database of your subconscious mind based on your experiences and conditioning. Those include beliefs from parents, teachers, siblings, friends, and early childhood experiences — all that you believe to be true. Your beliefs are recorded into your subconscious database and determined by your childhood influences. It is difficult to determine which influences made the most impact and created the most potential imprint to your subconscious mind. Once you become aware of the impact your subconscious programming has on your success, you will have the power to choose and create your responses more effectively.

Beliefs hold creative power and kick-start the creative process. I refer to beliefs as "generators" for their ability to provide definition and structure to our thoughts, feelings and actions. Beliefs generate, create, influence and determine success.

The Success Creator Cycle starts when a situation becomes observed, and an interpretation is made based on the belief, which creates a thought form. Thoughts are physical forms of your interpretation. The logic that has the power to transform and take action on the belief's intentions. Thoughts have creative power and generate feelings in the form of vibrations, just like a small seed that communicates your feelings to the world in the form of "frequencies." This frequency will either attract or repel your desired success depending upon the energetic state you use to generate it.

Feelings are creative energy in motion. They give juice to drive you toward achieving the outcomes you desire. Feelings are the vehicle that carry and propel you to the desired destination. They are the movement that transports your energy into action. Feelings generate the actions that take you toward success or away from success.

The actions generated by your feelings determine how and where you will focus your energy. Your ability to take action and carry out the beliefs, thoughts and feelings in a focused manner determines the results you achieve.

Like a grow light that is purposely directed at one specific rose bush instead of the mass of rose bushes surrounding it, the level of your success depends upon your ability to direct your energy with clarity, consistency and connectivity for achieving your goals and desires. You might wonder at this point, how does this all work?

How do we align the right thoughts, with the right feelings and right actions to increase our levels of *success*?
This is where Self-Management is key.

When we have clarity on the desired vision of success and identify the leadership success state of energy needed to produce the envisioned success, the next step is to identify the core beliefs necessary to propel the success forward.

Let's explore this idea further. Reflect upon your success statement created in the self-leadership section. Notice the energy that lives around what you truly want to accomplish. How can you create an energetic connection with this desire and attach the desired experience with one of the leadership success states to enhance your experience of success?

Now let's take this awareness to the next step. What beliefs might need to be true for you to feel fully engaged with this vision's success? What beliefs are necessary for you to feel that your vision is 100 percent possible to achieve? Spend a few moments exploring your beliefs around the desired vision of your success and capture a few beliefs that appear to have the most creative potential. This process requires you to view it from multiple perspectives, so you can fully understand its true potential and impact.

Once you have captured the beliefs, notice what thoughts they create. If you believe you *can* accomplish something instead of failing to achieve your desired success, notice the difference between the energies of the two outcomes. The difference lives in the beliefs that are driving the desire forward. As you work with how your beliefs create and impact your thoughts, notice what thoughts get activated. What feelings come to the surface? Just explore, be patient, and notice what's showing up. Observe which beliefs, thoughts and feelings have the most energy around them.

This process is a true art of creativity that takes practice, trust, and patience. However, if you stay with the process, you will use it endlessly to create long-term sustainable success. By identifying the core beliefs, thoughts and feelings that align with your desired goals, you will notice a personal buy-in that promotes positive action toward transforming your desires into your reality. Each time you work through this process you will automatically notice evidence of your desires becoming true. Just like a key aligns with the lock it is designed to fit, by aligning the right ingredients of beliefs-thoughts-feelings-actions together, this creative process opens the pathway to increased levels of success.

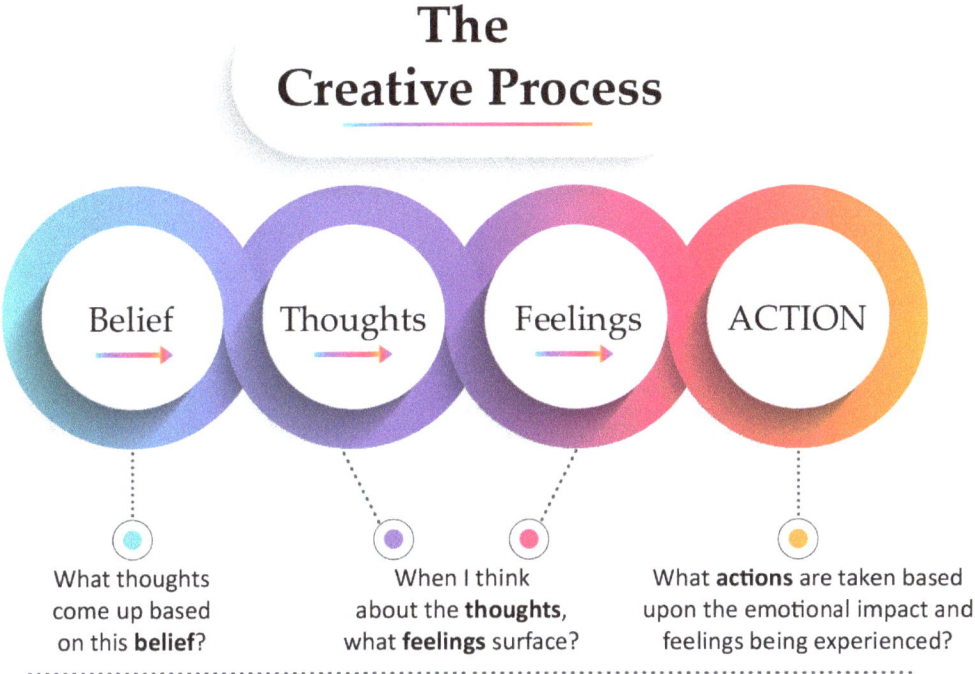

Inspired Discovery Exercise

Return to the ideal vision of success you created in the self-leadership module. Take a few moments to reconnect to this desire. Does this vision truly reflect the experience you most desire? As we connect with the "being state," it is often helpful to break down the success vision into smaller bits of awareness.

What exactly do you want to experience?

As you review your vision statement once again, try to break the vision into experiences. Vision statement examples follow.

- I want to experience like-minded people who share my passion for innovation at work.

- I want to spend at least four hours of my work week dedicated to researching latest technologies.

- I want to experience attending this year's technology conference to review the latest products and meet the distributors.

Break down your desired vision of success into a small grouping of experiences to promote clarity on your desired experiences, which are represented in your ideal vision-of-success statement.

Now, that you've defined the experiences that are being represented by your vision-of-success statement, review the seven states of leadership success and determine which one or more states are necessary to generate and create this vision. Consider who you need to be in each moment to align with the qualities you desire.

Does your vision require you to embody characteristics of the cheerleader, opportunist or creator state(s)? Which state(s) offer the energy needed to produce your vision?

Create a list of qualities and their associated leadership success states to promote more insight and application.

Practice this a few times with several goals until you get comfortable applying the success creation formula with each new goal. You may identify additional objectives to deepen your practice.

The sample thought process next will help you work through the creative process cycle for any desired outcome.

#1 **What is your ideal vision of success?**
    (List your desired result) _____

#2 **Which of the seven states of leadership success provides the most energetic impact to the desired vision?**
    Select specific state(s) and identify the primary thought-feeling-action that resonates with you.

    o Primary Thought: _____

    o Primary Feeling: _____

    o Primary Action: _____

#3 **What belief(s) will stimulate and solidify the desire to create this result?**

    Identify beliefs: _____

For example: if your goal is to get promoted to vice president in the next six months, you must first ask yourself: Is this true, do I believe this is possible? If your answer is yes, then perfect, you are in congruence. If your answer is no, and you don't believe this desire is possible, identify new beliefs until you resonate with a belief that is in congruence with your desire. Select the belief that leaves you feeling the energy of excitement or some higher level of success-oriented emotion.

#4 **Where's the evidence? What proof are you noticing that the creative process is working?**

As you continue to work through this process and become more comfortable with its application, remember to check in several times throughout the day to notice your current state of energy. Does your current state support and enhance your success or do you need to shift your awareness to a more empowering state? Are you creating from a place of success-building or success-blocking energy? What changes, if any, are required?

Your state of being is a creative process that harnesses the quality of energy needed to reach the desired outcomes of your goals and objectives.

Key questions to consider:

- What type of success am I creating in this moment?

- Do the current state of being and behaviors I'm expressing align with my desired experience of success or do they prevent or limit my success?

- Am I moving toward or away from my desired goals?

How to Create Your Leadership Success Style

Your state of being is the core creative substance you use to either create success or come up with stories about why you can't create success. It includes the quality of your present experience and reflects the current level of energy being used to generate the outcome you're experiencing. To create success, we must learn to harness the leadership success state that embodies the qualities of energy necessary to achieve the desired results.

In this chapter, my intention is to offer support and awareness on how to use the seven states of leadership success to create a leadership presence that supports your desired "being" state. Let's explore the "being" state further.

Our creative power and success-oriented energy lives in the moment, not reflected in the past or based on your visualizations of the future. We either plant seeds of success in each moment or we create stories about why success is not possible. In each moment of our awareness a "being" state offers unlimited potential. Whether we experience success is through individual choice; we have the power to choose how we will use our "being" state each moment of the day.

To fully understand this concept, let's review your primary tendencies and the way you most often create success. Primary tendencies are how you most often perceive and react to situations, events and circumstances you encounter every day. Consider a current situation you're going through at work and ask yourself, "Where does my energy live?" Which one of the seven leadership success states resonates most closely to my current experience?

Before we assess our energy and determine the success state that is being represented, try to recall your last visit for an eye exam. Let that memory be a metaphor for determining your leadership success state. Do you remember the last time you had your eyes tested when the optometrist used multiple lenses with multiple views to test your vision? Most often they ask you to select which lens provides the best vision. "Which is better, one or two? Two or three?" Sound familiar? "Which lens makes your vision most clear and which is fuzzy? Which lens makes the chart easier to read?"

Getting an eye exam and assessing your level of vision is similar to assessing your leadership success state.

Consider each leadership success state listed next. It may be helpful to envision each success state as a lens that provides a different view from all the other states. Notice the success state that speaks to you and provides the most energetic connection with how you routinely respond to situations. Review each statement listed below as if it is a "lens through which to see the world." Notice which state or "lens" offers you the best vision.

State # 7
Do I see the world through the Mastery Leadership State? Do I model absolute passion, abundance, freedom, fulfillment, self-confidence, ease and flow?

State # 6
Do I see the world through the Creator Leadership State? Am I intuitive, joyful, creative, non-judgmental, fearless, smiling with a sense of oneness?

State # 5
Do I see the world through the Opportunist Leadership State? Am I calm, confident, comfortable, authentic, peaceful and partnership-oriented?

State # 4
Do I see the world through the Cheerleader Leadership State? Am I caring, supportive, dedicated, accommodating, playful and sometimes out of balance?

State # 3
Do I see the world through the Status Quo Leadership State? Am I tolerant, calm, settling for less, rationalizing, playing it safe and secure with little or no uncertainty?

State # 2
Do I see the world through the Dominance Leadership State? Am I angry, stressed, judgmental, frustrated, disappointed, struggling and conflicted?

State # 1
Do I see the world through the Victim Leadership State? Am I fearful, self-doubting, lacking confidence, depressed, in survival mode, stuck?

You are living and leading primarily from one of these seven states. Take a moment and identify which state you live in most frequently. The energetic qualities associated with the leadership state you most often use to create success is your primary tendency, your potential for creating success. For this exercise, we will use a seven-point scale to depict the quality of energy being used to create your success. In this scale, the mastery state has a score of seven representing your full potential. This is a depiction of you at your absolute best potential for creating success. Each state below seven reduces in power and potential by one point. As an example, the creator state would be six points, the opportunist state would be five points and so forth.

Using this scale as a measurement of success, rate your current potential for creating success based upon the discoveries outlined above.

My current potential to create success measures ____ points.

What is the gap between your full potential for success that lives at the mastery state of seven points and your primary tendency state where you live at this moment?

Briefly write a description of where you are now, the experiences you're having at this moment related to your experience of success and compare it to your ideal vision of success. The space between your current and your desired experience defines the gap of success. This gap defines the opportunity, a pivot point for increased awareness that provides great insight, inspiration and increased potential. It is an invitation for shifting your attention to living from a new inspired state, the state I've defined as the Inspired Authentic Leader.

The Success Barometer

Once we have a clear vision of our current success compared to our desired success, we see the gap between those two experiences. The graphic above depicts the distance between our point A starting location (success now) and our point B desired destination (desired success). The gap identifies the journey, helps us consider the desired experience between point A and B and the steps we must take to ensure that we arrive at the right destination. Your gap of success is like a GPS system being used in an automobile to ensure that the driver takes the shortest, most direct path offering the optimal experience along the way.

As you create a visual of your own success barometer that defines your current experience of success or the lack of success in comparison with your desired success, ask yourself these questions:

- Are you creating your desired experience of success?

- Does the lack of success you're experiencing shape or define you?

Consider the qualities that define your current leadership presence and ask yourself, "Does the leadership state I live in most often have the potential to create the level of success I desire? If the answer to your question is yes, then you move forward toward increased levels of success. If, however, the response was no, then it is necessary to identify the state that offers the greatest momentum to create the success you desire. As you reflect on your current state, observe and acknowledge without judgment. Each leadership state offers its own unique experience and can be beneficial in different areas of life.

For a list of the seven leadership success states and their associated qualities, review the self-leadership descriptions in Section II as a reference. Identify the state that best resembles your thoughts, feelings and actions. This is who you are being, this is the energy you are using to generate success.

If you're not leading from the most empowering state of leadership, identify which state reflects the success potential you need to support your vision. Again, notice the thoughts, feelings and actions associated with the leadership success state to determine the optimal experience for alignment. Once you've identified the qualities that are associated with one of the seven leadership success states, continue your exploration in discovering ideas around how to connect with this new state. What experiences might promote the characteristics of this state and help you embrace its qualities more often? Who do you know who shows this desired leadership state as a behavior model?

As your awareness comes into alignment with the new leadership state, record your insights below.

Current Leadership State: _____

Desired Leadership State: _____

Each time you work through this process and observe the various qualities of who you are being, the awareness will support you in creating the desired leadership success state you need to excel. Capture a clear description of your current state before you read onward.

Your energetic presence captures who you are being and reflects the way you show up to life. The energetic space that your being creates, and the energy you bring to challenges, opportunities, dreams, and visions will define and determine your experience of success.

11. Communication that Creates or Deflates Success

Success is the integration of belief with behavior. You rise above the level of the problem to the level of the solution, from pain to potential, purpose, and power. As we continue to break down the many factors that create or control success, it is essential that we consider the impact of our communication and conversation with ourselves and others.

The Power of Words to Create or Deflate Success

Language and the words you use are forms of energy. Words are potential expressions that have the vibrancy to create or limit success. The verbiage you choose to describe experiences, ideas and situations will reveal your consciousness. Language announces what you believe to be true. Words are a creative process that define what you are speaking into existence.

Every statement you make and every question you ask reveals your values, attitudes and the way you perceive yourself and the world that surrounds you. Your thoughts and words both create; they build the foundation from which you experience the world.

You are in a creative state every moment that you use words to create your intentions and describe your experience of each situation. Words have the power to build success or block success. Take notice of the words you use to describe a situation. With which of the seven states of leadership success do your words resonate most often? (To refresh, refer to the chart in Chapter 8: The Seven States of Leadership Success.) Are you speaking from the victim state? Are you speaking from the dominance, status quo, cheerleader, opportunist, creator or master state? Carefully consider and continue to note which leadership success state best describes your routine conversations?

Notice the words you use to create success. Your language opens the door to your own self-perception and focuses your view of yourself and the world around you. Your language reveals the underlying patterns of why you experience limitation or unlimited success. How?

Your words contain seeds of greatness that can create success. It is important to take notice of words focused on the past that may reflect negatively on yourself and others.

The association with language as a direct connection to success may be a new concept for you to consider. However, it is essential to break down each core element of your language that either creates or limits success.

Using Language Through Empowering Questions to Create Success

The quality of your success depends upon the quality of your questions. How and where do you focus the use of your words? Are your words focused in the past, in the now or the future?

When you communicate your message to others, it is important to speak in the now. Being fully present with your energetic presence allows you to harness the highest expression of authenticity and inspiration. Speaking from a fully engaged powerful state creates maximized success and conveys your truth to others in a way they fully understand.

Noticing the intentions behind your communication is key for optimizing success. Intentions give meaning and context to your words, like giving them an extra jolt of energy to fuel a specific outcome. The quality of the energy determines the caliber of your success. Identify the energy embedded within each word, each expression, and all forms of communication. Catabolic words invite success-blocking experiences, anabolic words invite success-building experiences. Catabolic words decrease success; anabolic words increase success. Your words have power; choose them wisely.

Notice, also, the tone of your voice, the texture, impact, and how others perceive what you are saying. What silent messages are you communicating through the energy of your body, the way you express yourself through facial expressions and your body language. Does your body appear stiff, closed, protective or is your posture open, relaxed, comfortable and confident?

Understanding the true potential of your communication and its impact on your experience of success correlates with the way you communicate and how you express your intentions to others. When you use anabolic words and statements to communicate your intentions, combined with expressions that fully align your energy of intent with the energy of your expression, your language becomes a powerful way to optimize your potential for increased levels of success.

Expanding Your Presence with Power Words

When you elevate your language, you elevate every area of your life. Anytime you use power words, or words with higher vibrations of energy, you expand your presence and catapult your energy into an expanded state. In this expanded state, you experience individual success and also more connections with others.

Notice how you feel when you hear the tone of different words that are being used to convey an intention. Notice the impact you feel when someone uses the word *"hate"*. Do you feel an energetic charge, or a less than desirable experience? Experiment with the word *"love"* and notice if this word creates a feeling of ease or openness for you. What if someone talks about feeling fearful, angry or limited. Notice how you feel. Compare the energetic experience with the words *"being inspired"* or *"creative"* or *"unity"* or another high-vibrational word. Notice the shift in how you experience each word, the different sensations of being open or closed, expanded or constricted. You have the potential to experience the energetic impact that each word, sentence, intention, thought and other forms of expression have on your ability to create success.

Using anabolic power words adds energy, just like when you sip a protein shake or choose a healthy snack instead of getting a candy bar you're craving out of a vending machine. The protein shake adds energy while the processed sugar in the candy bar actually depletes your energy.

Inspired Discovery

The next time you experience yourself saying or thinking something that contains catabolic destructive energy, pause and restate the way you describe or experience the situation in a more anabolic, productive way. At first, changing this pattern might be difficult because you may be so ingrained to speak without reflecting on the true potential of what you wish to communicate.

If you find such "word watching" difficult, try thinking of yourself as your favorite actor practicing for their next role. Describe your thoughts and experiences with passion, using adjectives and fully empowering words in each part of your expression. This method offers a temporary solution to rid yourself of automatic habits programmed in the subconscious part of your brain. By practicing a pause, breath or break between your thoughts and your responses, you interrupt old patterns and generate new habits in choosing words carefully to describe each experience in ways that invite success.

As an example, "I hate my work life" transforms to, "I do, in fact, like some things about my work day." Notice the energy that lives within the context of each statement. The first sentence "I hate my work life" is rooted in a weighted energy that decreases the potential for experiencing success. The second sentence does not denote maximized energy, but it shows a form of anabolic productive energy that has the potential to grow and create success.

Create a list of words, phrases and sentences you use to describe your life experiences. Track the catabolic words, statements and phrases for each catabolic occurrence.
Identify a new anabolic way to express the same situation.

- **Catabolic Words = Success Blocking**
- **Anabolic Words = Success Building**

Empowering Conversions

An example of restating a comment to achieve an empowering conversion follows.

- *From:* **I hate my work life.**
- *To:* **There are parts of my work life I enjoy.**
- *Evidence:* **Look for evidence that your new belief is true or partially true.**

As you work through this exercise, it is important that you identify a way to shift the energy at the root of the expression. Shifting one word to another word driven by the same catabolic intention will not produce momentum. You must shift the energy in both the intention and the words being used to increase your level of success. Identify a new way to communicate the idea, then look for evidence that it is true. You must believe it is true for it to transform energy. If you identify a new word but don't believe the essence of what you are saying is true, your outcome will remain in a success-blocking state instead of a success-building state.

- *From:* _____
- *To:* _____
- *Evidence:* _____

In the next chapter, we consider the traits of creative leadership and increase awareness of four energy busters that can block success.

12. Creative Leadership – Uncovering the Four Energy Busters

Creativity is a fundamental element of leadership and your ability to create the right conditions for success to unfold.

In our work together, creative leadership comes into play with your ability to pinpoint the leadership success state that is necessary to generate your desired level of success. The first creative step is to identify how you react or respond to situations presented throughout your work day. I call this creative process *"mastery in the moment"* because it presents the opportunity to choose and create success through each experience in each moment. You maximize your potential in every moment, which contributes to increased levels of fulfillment and overall success.

Your ability to choose how to **respond instead of reacting** to a situation is essential to creating success. How you use your thoughts, feelings and actions to shape your destiny is vital for achieving your desired outcome. When you lead from a place of reaction, it limits your success, or your success is non-existing.

Responding shows leadership; reacting shows the absence of leadership.

When you take ownership and choose how to respond to each situation, you lead from an empowered state of success. Your ability to assess each situation and choose your response promotes success. If you allow circumstances to trigger a reaction without choosing your response, this process puts you into a place of disempowerment that limits your success. Responding is creative energy. Reacting is a resistive form of energy and a passive style of leadership instead of a proactive one.

On which side of creative leadership are you? Do you most often choose how you will respond to situations, creating and shaping each experience? Or do you find yourself most often putting out fires and getting triggered by life events?

The creative leadership awareness is being introduced in this self-management section and will continue to unfold in the self-mastery section.

THE POWER OF THE PAUSE

One option for developing your skills for Creative Leadership and responding instead of reacting to situations is through the awareness and powerful practice of the pause.

Notice the energy that lives within any situation presented. Notice how the energy makes you feel. Notice the tone of voice with which the words are spoken. Observe the body language of the person communicating to you. Does the situation have a relaxed or tense feel to it? Just notice each of the qualities of the situation you experience prior to responding. When you practice scanning the energy of all experiences, you learn how to pause, which naturally limits your reactions.

The goal is to strengthen your energy resources to create success instead of minimizing energy to combat situations that arise out of a reactive state.

Consider the following process of creativity starting with a situation stimulus that sparks a thought, which creates a feeling, then an action and an overall result. If the stimulus is success oriented, it will generate a response. However, if the stimulus is success-blocking, it often stimulates a reaction that functions as a trigger and is stimulated by a programmed past condition. To ensure that we maintain our energy reserves, we want to respond to each situation through choice instead of through a reaction that is stimulated by a triggered event. Each time a stimulus presents itself, pause and ask yourself, "Is this experience success-building or success blocking?"

The chart below shows an example of transforming success blocking to success-building statements with new evidence showing its potential for success.

Transform Success-Blocking to Success-Building

SITUATION:
It's Monday Morning and time to start a new work week.

What are several ways you can choose to perceive the situation using **success-building** qualities instead of **success-blocking**?

SUCCESS-BLOCKING THOUGHT:
I hate my work life, another week of the grind.

EVIDENCE:
Each time I think about how much I dislike my work experience, I feel sad and notice a headache is present.

ACTION:
I often call in sick or end up leaving work early.

SUCCESS-BUILDING THOUGHT:
There are several tasks that I actually enjoy doing at work, maybe I will start the week doing one of those.

EVIDENCE:
Each time I work on creating a presentation, I notice that time simply flies by and I truly enjoy the process.

ACTION:
I realize how much my creativity is important to me and look for opportunities to showcase it in my work.

Note the thoughts that surface with a particular situation. If the thought feels fearful, stressful, worrisome, combative or any other qualities associated with the destructive, catabolic leadership success state, pause to reassess your options for creating a more success-oriented experience. A catabolic success-blocking thought that is revised and converted to an anabolic success-building thought contains an empowering, energetic, success-producing outcome.

The Pause is the Pathway to Success

How does the pause become the pathway to success? As an example, a colleague informs you that he has been invited to speak at an upcoming conference you've been considering for some time. As he describes his enthusiasm for the upcoming event, you have thoughts of resentment that stimulate questions such as, "Why not me?" and "How could this have happened?" or "Why was I not offered this opportunity?" These questions activate your emotions, and you may feel a sense of anger, frustration or sadness. In this reactive state, you notice your energy is moving toward a disempowering experience and you desire to realign and redirect your energy to a new empowering place.

Once you notice you are headed toward or are already experiencing a triggered state, create a pause by taking a deep breath, visualizing a large red stop sign, or even saying the word pause quietly to yourself. It is important to plan and establish the practice of the pause each time you notice the first indicator of a reactive state. You may notice feeling alarmed, a heightened intensity of emotion or a desire to react quickly. These are just a few indicators that come up during a reactive state experience.

By interjecting a pause before you interpret a situation, you will create the space you need to choose your desired response. After a few deep breaths that pause your reactions, you feel more aligned with potential choices for how you want to respond.

Pausing provides a pathway to silencing the reactive state and uncovers the opportunity to decide how you will move forward. A simple pause offers a transformation, shifting from a disempowering state to an empowering state by acknowledging the need to stop the reactive state and regain control. Once you regain control and experience the calmness of the pause, you can decide how you would like to engage your energy with a response. This is the ideal time to explore the potential options you have for responding from a place of strength. At first, this transformation may take a little time, but as you practice sensing the energy of a reactive state and quickly converting it from a disempowering to empowering response, the process becomes automatic and success producing.

Let's continue with the example of the colleague invited to attend and present at a conference. As a leader who is responding from an empowered state, you might respond by offering your colleague congratulations, asking if there's an opportunity for you to help work on the presentation. It is possible to create a win-win situation in which your ideas are showcased, leaving you feeling valued and excited for your coworker's success. By using an empowering approach to leadership success, you partner with the opportunity of the potential that promotes unlimited possibilities to experience individual and combined success.

Each moment gives us the opportunity to create and experience success. The outcome we experience is shaped by whether we respond to a situation through choice or allow the situation to trigger us into a reactive state, an experience that limits our potential.

EMBRACING YOUR FULL CAPACITY TO CREATE SUCCESS

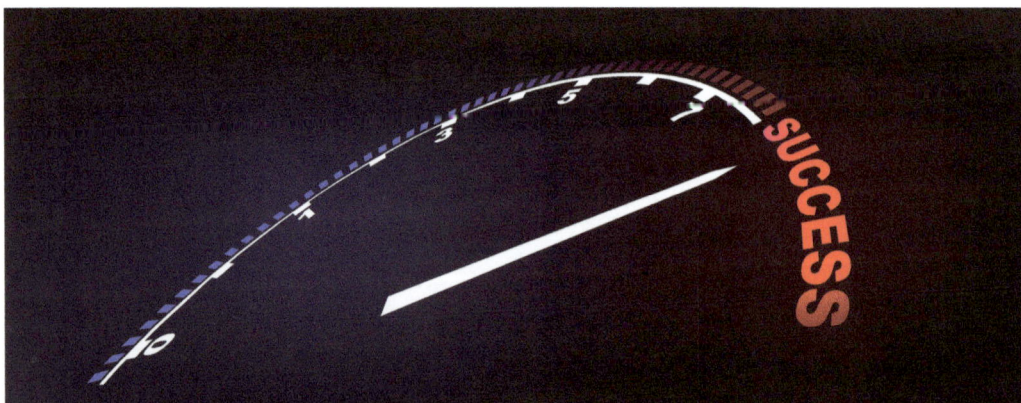

Success increases when you use your full capacity, your total engaged energy, to generate the outcome of your desires. You have 100 percent of your energy, power and capacity for success available to you. Imagine an automobile's fuel tank filled to maximum capacity for the travel ahead.

To visualize this potential, imagine your car's fuel gauge and notice the needle pointing to the "F" for full. Also notice the other indicators that represent a half-tank, and "E" for empty. There are a lot of potential indicators to define the capacity of your car's resources. When you fill your car's fuel tank, you have 100 percent pure capacity to travel toward your desired destination. Just like your car's potential, you also have 100 percent of your energy to use as a resource to fuel your efforts for creating success. The challenge is not that you don't have enough capacity; the limiting factor is how well you use the resources you have. In the example of an automobile, this might be reflected as wasting a portion of your fuel to drive around aimlessly without a true destination, instead of saving your fuel to get to a high priority destination or desire.

The deciding factor depends on the percentage of success-building energy you use to create success compared to the success-blocking energy used to hinder success. Do you focus and direct your energy toward meeting desired goals or does a portion of your energy get redirected to another task, weakening and distracting your ability to excel fully?

Using the qualities associated with the seven leadership success states that are success-building instead of success-blocking will maximize your ability to achieve success. However, if you use qualities associated with leadership states that are success-blocking such as fear, frustration, anger, control and self-importance — to mention a few — you limit success and only use a small portion of your capacity and potential to achieve your goals.

Returning to the analogy of an automobile, consider success building as the potential to shift into a high-performance gear with increased potential for performance. In the success-blocking state, success is limited, and the car runs in a slower-performing state with less potential. Just like a speed governor device that limits your speed of performance, using success-blocking qualities limits your potential to excel. Think of driving with one foot on the brake pedal while you are trying to accelerate.

While considering the leadership success states being success-building or success-blocking, note the percentage of energy that is being used to create or prevent success. It is vital to understand where the primary conflicts exist. As an Inspired Authentic Leader, you will have a keen ability to manage your leadership success state. You will create success-building experiences associated with creativity, inspiration, service, joy, ease, flow and other positive qualities. These are opportunities for new patterns to become your new habits.

If you are not experiencing the level of success you desire, it's because a portion of your energy is being limited, constricted, and not being used in a productive success-building way.

Are Energy Busters Blocking Your Success?
The Four Energy Busters — Roadblocks to Success

There are four primary reasons you are not experiencing your desired level of success — **The Four Energy Busters.**

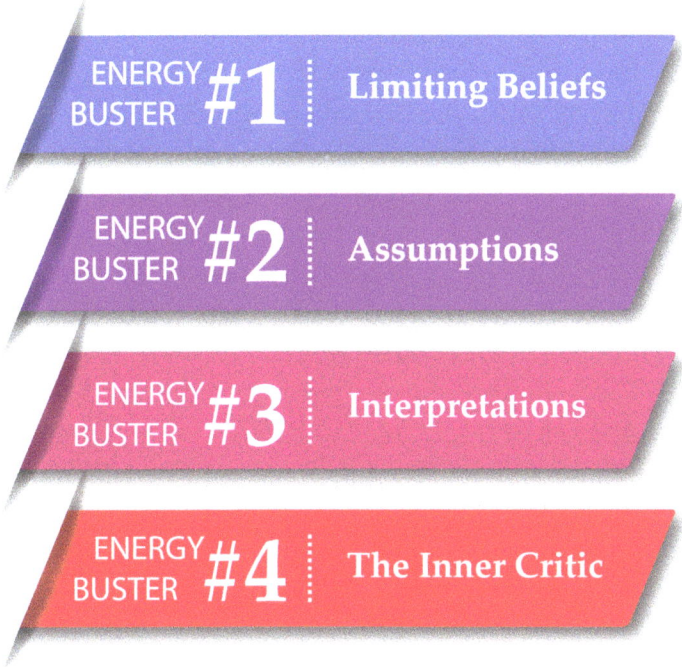

Energy busters carry a weight comparable to a heavy ball and chain wrapped around your wrist, preventing you from feeling free, creative, inspired and fully engaged. As an example, imagine you have an important project due and you feel eager to get started. You are ready to capture your thoughts, ideas and creative energy to ensure that you produce a quality product. Your excitement and energy levels are high as you brainstorm the true potential for this new project.

As you begin work on this project, you notice lots of loud noise in your local surroundings and realize a large group of coworkers are holding their afternoon conversation close to your workspace.

They are enjoying time together, laughing, telling stories and sharing experiences. However, the magnitude of the noise disrupts your focus and prevents you from fully concentrating on your project. Each time you engage more deeply, a new burst of noise distracts you and you begin to feel frustrated and angry. Notice how this might impact your ability to produce a quality product with these distractions surrounding you.

In this situation, the way you perceive the situation and how you interpret its meaning will determine your success potential. If you respond to this situation as "oh, this is just Bob doing what he does, goofing off for 15 minutes before he ends his work day," then the impact may be minimum. But what happens if the loud noise gets under your skin and you are no longer in a response state? Instead of responding appropriately, you are now in full-blown reaction mode, with thoughts like "how rude, don't they understand that some people are trying to work around here?" If this is your reaction, then most likely your creative energy will be redirected to the reaction taking place instead of your desired project outcome. Can you relate to a similar circumstance when you've desired to complete a task only for your energy and awareness to be hijacked by something outside your control?

This is an example of an energy buster based upon an interpretation of a situation that is draining and reduces a portion of your creative energy. It prevents you from using your energy to engage, create and shape your ideas so they are optimized into a quality product that reflects your desired vision of success.

Each of the four energy buster experiences creates a core conflict that either limits or prevents success.

Let's explore them together.

ENERGY BUSTER #1 | **Limiting Beliefs**

"Limiting Beliefs are false messages about our self. They are like dark shadows hiding in our nature"
—Dr. Deepak Chopra

Limiting beliefs are also beliefs you have about the world, about others, about situations in life that hold you back from experiencing success. Beliefs align and focus energy toward success or limit and decrease energy that impacts success. Beliefs are at the forefront of the creative process that generates success. As mentioned in previous chapters, what you believe to be true and "buy into" will determine how you respond or react. Beliefs kick-start the thoughts, feelings and actions, which either generate success or create challenges that prevent success.

If you believe something is true, you will feel empowered and inspired, directing your energy and full capacity toward it. However, if you believe something is not true, you will most likely avoid taking actions toward its fulfillment. Even if you do take action, you likely will not devote as much energy toward achieving the success you desire.

Examples of Limiting Beliefs

- It's impossible to have fun at work.
- Work life is never easy.
- To get promoted you must start at the bottom and work your way up the ladder.
- There's no place for workplace creativity and authenticity.

Transforming Limiting Beliefs

As soon as you realize that a belief is disempowering and preventing success, start the transformation by identifying the primary belief that is limiting your success.

- **Identify the primary belief.**
  What is the belief at the root of the experience?
- **Assess its validity.**
  Explore the belief's origin. What evidence do you have that it's true? Is it possible that another belief is equally true?
- **What is the impact?**
  Determine the impact the belief is having on your desired success. Is it success-building or success-blocking? Imagine the belief is being weighed on a tipping scale. How much would it weigh? Would it lean toward success or away from it?
- **Creating a new belief.**
  What new belief would be more productive, more empowering and fueled by success-building energy? Sometimes, you can use the original belief and choose the opposite of that belief, replacing its blocking potential with building potential.

Imagine you have a belief such as, "they do not design work to be fun," and you're tired of leaving the work day feeling frustrated, unfulfilled and burned out. How does this belief serve you? What might your workplace experience be like if you created new beliefs? An example of a more empowering belief is "My work life gives me a feeling of contribution" or "My work gives me the opportunity to express myself and share my gifts with others."

Choose an empowering belief that resonates with you. You have the power to choose your beliefs; they are not hardwired. It only requires a decision to transform one belief into a new belief that is more productive, empowering and success-oriented.

Create a new belief that energizes your spirit and shifts you into a more productive and energetic state. Beliefs are decisions we have made along the way, information we have given meaning to and used to create our experiences. We can assess each belief and determine if it creates success or blocks success. Creating new beliefs can stimulate and excite; they invite new awareness and increase enthusiasm that presents new opportunities and insights. As you experiment with different beliefs and determine which ones will represent the truth for you going forward, notice the ones that feel the most energizing.

When you choose a new belief to accept as a partner, you may feel immediate shifts in your physical, mental, emotional and spiritual energy.

ENERGY BUSTER #2 : Assumptions

An assumption is a belief that because something happened in the past, it will happen again. Assumptions are more personal than the limiting beliefs previously discussed, and assumptions have more energy associated with them. Assumptions are based on past conditioning. If you believe something won't work, you won't feel motivated to take the actions toward achieving it. This assumption might include experiences you recall about a situation in the past that didn't turn out the way you planned. You mentally attached a label to this experience, and it became programmed in the subconscious part of your brain.

Let's consider a scenario that exemplifies an assumption. An employee submits a resume for a new position and is unsuccessful in being selected as the right candidate. This experience might impact the person's ability to feel hopeful the next time a new opportunity is available, based on the association with the past failure to succeed. The assumption impedes the employee's ability to experience success and prevents taking actions to pursue new goals.

Transforming Assumptions

Assumptions are based most often on personal experiences and can be difficult to transform. Ask yourself this primary question: Just because something happened in the past, is it true that the same outcome must happen again?

Reflect on the assumption you wish to challenge and consider a time when you experienced a similar situation that created an event that was success-oriented. Look for evidence that someone else experienced the opposite of your assumption. Ask yourself, "If they experience success in this situation what prevents me from also experiencing success?"

The idea is to challenge the assumption and identify other potential truths that can shift the perception of the assumption.

Revisit the areas of your life in which you want to experience success and notice if any of these areas are being blocked by an assumption. If so, use the questions listed above to shift the assumption and transform it into a new success-oriented belief.

ENERGY BUSTER #3 | Interpretations

An interpretation is the opinion you create about a situation or experience. You create a story about a situation you believe to be true and search to identify evidence to add strength to the story. However, your interpretation is only one possibility out of many, it is a single viewpoint that keeps you focused upon a state of limited-to-no success.

Question the interpretation and notice if it is success-building or success-blocking? Explore other potential viewpoints that might also apply to the same situation.

Ask yourself these questions:

- What is the opposite way of viewing this situation?
- What's another way to interpret this?
- How might other people interpret the situation?
- Which interpretation promotes success?

Consider using the seven states of leadership success to view the situation from each of the seven perspectives. Imagine that you have seven different pairs of glasses and they are all different colors. Select a pair to view the victim state of leadership success and notice what you see. Select another pair and view the dominance state and notice your experience from this viewpoint. Now try on another pair of glasses that represent the status quo state of leadership. What's different from this perspective? How is your interpretation of the experience different? Do this for each of the seven states of leadership success and identify the potential states that create the most favorable level of success. This exercise deepens our awareness on the importance of perspectives. Our experience of success depends upon how we view a situation, what we believe to be true.

If you are not experiencing the level of success you desire, consider viewing the situations through a new lens or a new interpretation of what you believe to be true, and notice if the new experience differs.

ENERGY BUSTER #4: The Inner Critic

We all have an inner critic living in the background of our awareness and functioning as a traffic cop to keep us safe. This inner critic leaps into action when it perceives a danger or when we are considering something new that we haven't experienced before. The inner critic's job is to keep us informed; its trust is limited to the known experiences that are safe. Its primary role is to prevent us from taking chances with new experiences or taking actions that are unknown. The inner critic communicates to us through the sound of our inner voice, a subtle conversation that talks to us throughout the day to ensure we stick to the most reliable, safe and secure path.

The inner critic holds the most intense emotional charge of the four energy busters. When it communicates to you, it is very difficult not to pay attention. Its communication might include statements such as:

- You better not take that sabbatical, you will never get your job back when you return, and you might not get any job.

- You better not speak up at the sales meeting and draw attention to yourself, you will only embarrass yourself.

- You know you're not smart enough to do that new job, right?

- You can't apply for that new job, they will find out that your skills are not sufficient.

These statements are only a few of many that the inner critic might use to convince you that you are not good enough, safe enough or in some way lacking.

Transforming Your Inner Critic

The first step to transforming your relationship with your inner critic is to acknowledge it. Develop a personal relationship with it instead of viewing it as something to resist. Realize that it has a job to do, which is to keep you safe and that is an important role. Once you acknowledge and create a partnership with it, you will notice that the inner critic loses its intensity and strength.

Another way to transform the inner critic is to respond to it. Each time it advises you on a situation, come up with a response that allows it to feel understood. This planned response might be something like, "I hear you loud and clear and understand that you have concerns, but don't worry, I've got this, and I appreciate you giving me a heads up." The inner critic wants to know it's heard, acknowledged and valued. Once you work with it and even consider giving it a name of reference, it will reduce the intensity to one of support, rather than survival out of fear.

Leaders Are Inspired and Incredible

Your ability to acknowledge and bring energy to each of the four energy busters is key for creating success. If you have difficulty remembering the four energy busters, create a phrase that brings them to mind. I use the phrase "Leaders Are Inspired and Incredible" to bring to mind the four energy busters. In the word "Leaders" the "L" stands for "Limiting Beliefs." The letter "A" in the word "are" reminds you of "Assumptions." The "I" in the word "Inspired" stands for "Interpretations," and the "I" in the word "Incredible" stands for the "I" in The Inner Critic. Essentially, the phrase, "Leaders Are Inspired and Incredible" adds energy, strength and power to each of the four energy buster principles. If this idea doesn't work for you, consider a symbolic item that has a reminder message that will keep you aware of the limited energy of the four energy busters. With practice, you will be able to transform each energy buster that shows up in any experience.

If you are a creative person, gather a few beads, inspirations, or other items and craft your own bracelet, necklace, desk décor or another item you can keep nearby. Use your creativity and anchor your awareness for overcoming the limiting power of each of the four energy busters. In this way, you will effectively transform them into a position of increased potential.

THE IMPACT OF CATABOLIC SUCCESS-BLOCKING ENERGY ON WELL-BEING AND SUCCESS

Throughout the Self-Management section, we've focused on how to optimize our potential to create success. I have broken this goal down to identify the core qualities that contain the most vibrant potential in the moment and to assess the creative energy that is being used to generate success.

The most successful leaders in the world have mastered the ability to manage their leadership state so it is directed and aligned with the greatest potential for success.

It is essential to assess the energetic impact of success and realize that every energetic action has an energetic consequence to it. That means every belief, thought, feeling, action or response has a specific influence on whether or not you experience success.

Essentially, there is a cost impact associated with how you respond to each situation. The cost impact can influence many areas of your life. Your well-being, financial state, relationships, personal fulfillment, advancement, health and many other life components depend upon your ability to create success.

One of the greatest threats to your well-being is stress-related illness. Stress is based on how you perceive a situation; it is your response to a circumstance, event or situation. Your response includes how you perceive it, interpret it and assign meaning to the situation that kick starts the sequence of thoughts, feelings and actions determining the outcome. Unfortunately, you may have gotten into a vicious loop of being triggered hundreds of times throughout the day by using the subconscious part of your mind to identify a situation as a perceived threat rather than a true life-threatening incident.

To deepen your understanding of the critical impact that stress plays on your well-being, let's explore the true nature of stress. Stress increases your energy demands. When you are not living in a stress state, your body generates anabolic hormones. These hormones heal the body, build tissue, and generate cells. This allows the body to optimize itself. As a result, it's easier to maintain a solution focus and feel energized. It propels you forward to new possibilities and opportunities. In a healthy state the mind perceives that the environment is safe and supportive, and it preoccupies the cells with the growth and maintenance of the body.

In stressful situations, your body goes into survival mode and the growth processes become restricted or suspended in a stressed system. The cells forego their normal growth functions and adopt a defensive, protective posture. It diverts the body's energy resources normally used to sustain growth to protective systems that are activated during periods of stress.

While your system can accommodate periods of acute, brief stress, prolonged or chronic stress is debilitating. Its energy demands interfere with the required maintenance of the body and often lead to illness.

What are some of the changes you experience during periods of stress? Routinely, the blood pressure elevates, adrenaline levels rise, the pupils dilate to improve the field of vision, cortisol production suppresses your immune system, inflammation increases in the body and compromises your immune systems. Long-term stress can lead to many diseases, such as diabetes, a condition in which insulin production in the body is blocked, and low-grade inflammation exists. Stress programs the body for impact to protect and survive; it doesn't decipher between real danger and situations that are triggered by a reaction state.

Your ability to minimize stress and secure your resources for true life-saving experiences is key to ensuring your maximized success. Pause for a moment and imagine the impact of your body's resources if it undergoes several jolts of shock, or quick response reactions several times a day, forcing your body into a trauma state of preparation. If you are consistently triggering your physical, emotional, mental, and spiritual self into a threat-state experience, what happens to your desire to feel inner peace, joy, ease, flow and positive feelings that are associated with being successful. These emotions are all reduced or non-existent because the primary energy resources are being used to combat a perceived threat.

These stress-induced responses in your body can be compared to a large team of firefighters who are called repeatedly to combat massive fires only to discover the fire never existed. In this example, consider the impact of all the fire trucks, life-saving equipment and highly skilled personnel being allocated to the perceived threat, depleting most of their resources. When you use your energy to respond to a situation or perceived crisis that is not a true crisis, you decrease your energy and capacity to excel. You no longer have the required resources to achieve your goals. In some situations, once you deplete your energy reserve, you may not have the necessary energy to combat true threats that require your most vital resources. Therefore, you must have the tools and techniques in place to identify quickly if a situation is a perceived threat or truly a life-threatening situation. Ultimately, you must learn to optimize your strengths and energy to align with your desired outcomes under normal circumstances and maintain the potency of your energy reserves for combating true life-threatening situations.

In the next chapter, we explore moving beyond traditional states of leadership into empowered, authentic leadership for maximized success.

13. From Traditional to Authentic Leadership

As we mentioned in the beginning chapters of this book, I believe today's leaders are searching for ideas and strategies that will support them in moving beyond traditional forms of leadership and into authentic leadership—past the limitations of the victim, dominance and status quo leadership states. Today's leaders are eager to experience a new state of leadership that helps them to feel inspired and authentic. I call this new level of leadership a state of self-mastery known as the Inspired Authentic Leader.

At this renewed state of leadership, working professionals feel empowered, inspired and fully aligned with whom they are as individuals and collectively as primary contributors to their teams and organizations. They show increased self-awareness with an understanding of their purpose, passion and increased potential. They have the skills and discipline to align their focus and resources toward the goals of their desires combined with the awareness of their personal motivation that is driving their actions toward success. These leaders seek authenticity and are aligned with their true nature. They have a burning desire for greater levels of success and are fueled with passion, purpose and a willingness to step outside their comfort zones. They desire to experience self-mastery as a journey toward true authenticity, with heightened contribution, connection, inspiration and impact.

Let's break this down so it's easy to see the nuances that exist between traditional forms of leadership and authentic states of leadership. Understanding the seven states of leadership success can offer invaluable insight into the leader's journey and identify the turning point in a leader's career.

Traditional forms of leadership range between the victim state in level one to the status quo state in level three. You might have had the luxury of experiencing leaders who have expanded their awareness and have shown the ability to lead from an advanced state of leadership success, such as the cheerleader state, opportunist state, creator state or mastery state. Your opportunity is to transform your leadership awareness to evolve and embrace a state of self-mastery, which I call the Inspired Authentic Leader. When you embrace the vision of greatness and aspire to lead from the cheerleader, opportunist, creator and mastery states, you experience both internal and external levels of success. A true experience of success that is deeply fulfilling emerges and opens a pathway for living and leading from your greatest potential.

With this vision of success in mind, let's revisit the overall impact of the traditional catabolic and authentic anabolic forms of leadership to discover their deepest insights.

Traditional Leadership and Authentic Leadership

The primary distinguishing factor between traditional forms of leadership and authentic leadership is conscious awareness of oneself and the ability to lead from a place of increased potential.

When you lead from a traditional leadership approach, often your focus is on self-success and you may not consider the impact you have on others. As a traditional leader, you:

- May not view yourself as part of a greater whole
- Often settle for the status quo state of leadership, experiencing limited visions of success
- Frequently view success with a mentality that "good is good enough"
- May not aspire to achieving a state of self-mastery. You may experience leadership from a place of pain or frustration instead of desire and motivation, often feeling as if you "have to, need to, must do" something instead of "want to, choose to, like to" do something
- Build your skills from a traditional view of leadership, often experiencing triggered reactions and less-than-desirable work environments
- Rarely entertain the power of pause and the importance of taking ownership over choices made from a planned response to situations instead of reacting from a triggered state
- May hide behind a false identity that is disconnected from your core values and begin to direct your success focus toward external, tangible goals instead of internal, intangible goals
- Often lead with only your mind instead of combining the mind-body-spirit (holistic) leadership perspective
- Use traditional approaches to leadership, routinely hitting plateaus in your success level

Why? This pattern continues because you haven't yet considered the full impact of not being present and centered in your own state of natural strengths, inner power and profound inner wisdom.

These character traits and qualities represent some of the differences that exist between traditional roles of leadership success and authentic leadership success. Once you begin to apply the opportunities of authentic leadership, you will realize the potential is enormous.

As you continue to reflect on the potential of traditional and authentic leadership success, the seven states of leadership success model will become a true "eye-opener." This model provides the depth of awareness to depict the actual experiences one might discover in each leadership practice. Each state, with its associated qualities and perspectives, provides keen insight on the impact and overall potential outcome of each leadership presence. This is where the true power of leadership surfaces, in learning to manage the state of energy to **lead from a success-building state instead of success-blocking state.**

Individuals who lead with the energy of the victim and dominance states of leadership success are leading in a catabolic, destructive success-blocking state of awareness. And this is most often where you will experience the stress impact. When individuals live in a repeated pattern of daily stress in these states, they can no longer live in a healthy rhythm. They move into a disharmonious state where stress, illness and disease often originate. In this state, our bodies no longer have the resources they need to sustain a healthy presence and lack the vibrancy required to prevent illness or disease.

The victim and dominance states of leadership success, and the qualities associated with them, keep the focus on the pain or the problem. The awareness of where energy lives in each moment is the first step to bringing the body back into homeostasis, a healthy balanced state. This balanced state embodies the resources and capacity needed to generate the ideal vision of success.

The Victim State Is Success-Blocking

To review, the victim state is the lowest state of the seven states of leadership success model explained in previous sections. It is a crisis state of leadership with little to no real leadership taking place. The leader in this experience has either experienced prior great success and has encountered a challenge that triggers them into the victim state or is an individual who lacks the self-confidence needed to take on a leadership role.

There are individuals in the workplace today who lack the self-leadership skills to define their vision of success. They often look to others to lead them and take ownership of their survival and sustainment in their daily roles, with little to no self-leadership. In my experience of working with many seasoned professionals, I often identify this energy with leaders who have experienced marked levels of success but now find themselves up against some challenge or hurdle. These challenges put them into a triggered state of feeling unworthy or lacking the skills and awareness to regain their momentum toward a success-building strategy. I see this experience of leadership when a leader has been overlooked for a promotion or released from a position they've been in for an extended period of time. Regardless of whether the release was due to cutbacks, funding issues, or performance challenges, leaders who perceive a lack of success in the past can sprout doubt about their ability to create success in the future. This experience puts them into a victim, success-blocking state. The longer they remain in the victim state, the more stuck and limited they become. This is a constricted state of leadership with limited awareness on what to do and how to take action. If they remain here for an extended period of time, they often experience signs of health issues or disease that adds to their list of challenges.

The real value here to understand is that every leader will experience setbacks, unexpected challenges, and limited success at times. It's not uncommon to feel the victim energy on occasions. However, the powerful game changer to leadership is realizing when you are experiencing the victim state and having the awareness and skills you need to shift quickly to a higher state of leadership success.

The Dominance State Is Success-Blocking

A vibrant experience of energy, the dominance state is where the majority of today's leaders live. It can be a place of great purpose and passion, but the focus is on the self instead of the project, team, corporation or others. It is a state of self-success at the cost of all others. Leaders who use this energy to lead can often accomplish increased levels of success by dictating their expectations to others and demanding their needs be met. In this state of leadership, you might experience micro-managers who feel they have to oversee every aspect of a colleague's work, impose extreme deadlines and numerous requirements that create a lot of stress and tension. The environment will be more of a top-down approach to leadership with each coworker having little to no input into the outcome or unique role as an individual contributor. This leadership role may also include aspects of struggling, blaming, resentment, competition, frustration, conflict, arguing, disappointment, and similar negative and counterproductive emotional qualities.

The dominance state of leadership often leads to a high level of employee turnover, lack of employee engagement, limited productivity, lower profits and an overall lower level of fulfillment. Although the leader might be successful in getting coworkers to meet their objectives out of fear of losing their jobs, or some other concern, success at this leadership state is extremely limited and is not productive for extended periods of time. This is the work setting where employees get burned out, call in sick, take extensive vacation days and generally feel unhappy. These are a few of the challenges inherent in a work environment directed by an individual who leads from a dominance state of leadership.

Some of the dominance state descriptors might seem to be too harsh to apply to your work situation. Consider assessing your situation more closely to identify similar qualities that relate to the traits described. It is vital to pinpoint these factors because they reduce the capacity and energy you need to create optimal success. Any success-blocking patterns drain energy and limit your success and the success of your team.

Once you have practices in place to minimize and rid yourselves of the effects of victim and dominance states of success, you decrease the triggers, stress, and energy that has been blocking your path to optimal success. As you manage your energy and direct it toward success-building qualities, you increase your well-being and overall success, regardless of how you define success.

The Status Quo State Is *Success-Building*

Tendencies of both the catabolic and anabolic energy states are evident in the status quo state of leadership success. This state of leadership is the pivot point to leadership success, a place of opportunity in which self-leadership and self-responsibility show up in increased levels of awareness. It is the bridge of awareness and action between the catabolic (success-blocking) and the anabolic (success-building) states of success. Although the focus remains on the individual self, the energy of this state is centered upon rationalizing situations, settling for the status quo, or a belief that "good is good enough."

Leaders at this level are masters of the coping mechanism. The status quo leader also resonates with the anabolic energy, they are positive and productive, living in the world of solutions instead of problems. Leaders at this level choose their responses instead of reacting. When a crisis or challenge arises, they'll move to resolve it with confidence, responding with logic, instead of reacting with emotion.

This state of leadership success is the springboard for shifting success from a place of limitation to limitless potential by implementing the process of focusing the energy in a success-building state of awareness. As you embrace the potential of the status quo leadership success and continue to build momentum through the other four anabolic states, you have the tools and strategies in place to experience maximized success.

When leaders arrive at the experience of this state, they are often at a turning point in their careers and faced with the decision on whether to step forward into their authenticity and true purpose or to step back into the safety net of their traditional leadership role. They question whether to continue in the same leadership fashion that keeps them safe and secure living in the status quo or to take the leap and explore their true gifts, talents, desires and authentic skills.

The status quo leadership success state contains the energy of choice for two distinct views between opportunity and predictability. This is the point in most leaders' careers when they feel the inner desires for something more. They think about a change; they are at a turning point in their career after arriving to a comfortable place of living and leading in the win column for many years.

Leaders at this state have experienced some measure of success that provides a sense of personal confidence, security and status. On the other side of the confidence, they are also feeling a deeper yearning for something more, often not knowing what that "something more" is. They are feeling many of the spiritual qualities of wanting to contribute in a greater way, to experience a sense of freedom from their position's structure, to which they have become accustomed. They are wondering what it might feel like to be creative and express themselves in a more profound way. These individuals may desire to master their life's craft, and experience something new that has more personal fulfillment. They may join forces for a greater cause and contribute in such a way that makes a greater impact on the lives of others. Individuals often look for more purpose, passion, and a way to expand and express their true potential or the opportunity to explore their talents in a more profound way.

The status quo leadership success state invites leaders to pause and question what's next. During this time of inner reflection, leaders often make one of two choices: 1) they identify a plan to explore their inner callings and take the path less traveled to experience their authenticity and true nature or 2) they realize that they are not willing to take the risk to live or lead in the unknown and prefer to stick with the norm. The leader who chooses the traditional response to leadership values the comfort of the traditional leadership's safety net, justifying that the risk of embracing change is too great. It is the ultimate decision to continue the path of traditional leadership or embrace a renewed spirit for authentic leadership. The leader who heeds the call of the authentic leadership embraces the unknown and is eager to experience their vision of greater success.

Leaders who live and lead in the safety zone often rationalize their decisions based on fear from past experiences, and they settle into a comfortable place of the status quo. It is a place that is predictable, with a structure that allows them to feel the security and protection they need to excel.

Another key factor of the status quo leadership success state is that it's the home for self-leadership. When leaders experience this state, they take on ownership and full responsibility for their success; they realize their satisfaction and fulfillment depends on their choices inside and outside their work day. As the home of self-leadership, this state is built upon self-responsibility, self-direction and self-success. The self-leadership role signifies when leaders take on their own personal role of creating success. They are skilled at managing their energy and responses to overcome the triggers experienced in leaders that live and lead from the victim and dominance states. This is the state of choice, where each leader aspires to overcome conflict, maintain peace, and avoid confrontation. Each leader must choose how they create and experience success. Will they stick to the basics of traditional success or will they align their focus toward a new journey of self-realization? This state is fueled by the energy of their choice for traditional leadership versus authentic leadership, the choice to focus energy toward success-building versus success-blocking, and the choice to take on deeper levels of leadership awareness and be rid of the limiting success often experienced in the victim and dominance states of leadership.

Can you relate to a time in your career when you experienced the deeper inner calling of authentic leadership, desiring something more? How did you respond? Take notice of this awareness and increase your clarity on what the inner calling was guiding you to do. Do you still feel times when your spirit tells you to take another path? Deep dive into this awareness and allow it to unfold peacefully. Ask the questions, "What if?" and "Why not?" Listen closely to what wants to happen. Just notice and take no action initially. This is a practice of reflection and inquiry, an invitation to make peace with the part of you that is yearning to become more authentically aligned with your true nature of purpose, passion and increased potential.

Authentic leadership and traditional leadership both offer some level of reward and success-oriented experiences. Individuals must decide the right path to take based on personal values and their vision for success. Traditional leadership provides the security and safety for limited potential. Authentic leadership is a state of self-mastery that is aligned with unlimited increased potential. I call this self-mastery state the Inspired Authentic Leader.

Authentic leadership opens the door to uncovering the fabric of the leader's true nature and to gain insight into how best to respond when the going gets tough. It offers the chance to experience leadership skills and life from the most expanded perception of personal and professional expression.

Authentic leadership is an experience of self-mastery that focuses solely on the journey ahead instead of being attached to a final destination. There are no guarantees in the experience along the way. This journey requires boldness to shift from the safety net of the status quo to embrace the desire to live, lead, and fall in love with the higher states of leadership. Authentic leadership tests current beliefs, perceptions, and limited awareness, expanding to a new way of viewing the world. Authentic leadership opens the door to an experience of greatness that is routinely not experienced in traditional forms of leadership.

When leaders feel empowered and identify opportunities to combine their external success with internal awareness, they play a new game of leadership.

EXPLORING THE SUCCESS-BUILDING STATES OF LEADERSHIP

With increased clarity on the states of leadership that limit and prevent success, it's time to fully explore and understand the leadership states that evoke success and invite new opportunities to be exceptional.

The following review describes the four success-building states and their energies, which are productive, building, enhancing and sustainable. They offer leaders the experience of physical, mental, emotional, and spiritual wellness. These leadership states do not lead from positions of stress, tension, anxiety or the need to compete. These leadership states promote unity, authenticity, inner peace, respect, gratitude and all the key elements required to experience a sense of wellness, inner peace and balance. They each open the door to increased potential and success that combines both the internal and external factors of success.

▮ *Cheerleader State*

In your workplace, have you ever noticed a person who is filled with energy and uses it to support the needs of others? You may discover this person in the center of groups of people, focused on service, support and ensuring the success of others. You might also remember a person in your work environment who routinely walks around the office greeting everyone and trying to cheer them up. Cheerleader state leaders exhibit a keen compassion for others, showing appreciation, caring, gratitude, playfulness and similar supportive qualities.

The cheerleader state is a success-building state of leadership success. These leaders align well with the intangible qualities of leadership. Their primary focus is on others, rather than self. This is a powerful leadership state when it is balanced between focusing on others and maintaining appropriate self-leadership awareness. Cheerleader state leaders often use the term "we" instead of "I" in routine conversations and perspectives. This shift in focus opens the door for more authenticity and success-building energy. Those who lead from the cheerleader state inspire and support others to increased levels of fulfillment and success.

Although this is a great state of energy for any leader to experience, it's often not sustaining or long-term, unless the leader has the awareness and daily practice of balancing self-care and compassion with the care and support offered to others. Another challenge that often presents itself at this state, is when leaders assume that other individuals need or want their support when, in fact, they often don't. Leaders with this level of energy often make assumptions that they have the right answers and don't allow others the opportunity to explore their own ideas and opinions, resulting in conflict. Therefore, the goal of the cheerleader state of leadership is to ensure balance between self-success and others' success. That balance is achieved by self-management, the hub for analyzing strengths, weaknesses and the willingness to engage in support for self as well as others.

The cheerleader state best represents the home for self-management. Cheerleader state leaders demonstrate a willingness to support the success of others. They also must hone their skills in managing their energy, so they are able to create success for others without sacrificing their own success. It is essential for the cheerleader to maintain that leadership balance to ensure long-term success. If leaders direct too much of their energy toward helping others and neglect fulfilling their own personal success goals, they become frustrated, angry, overwhelmed and even stressed, all traits related to success-blocking energy rather than the success-building energy they desire.

Opportunist State

A success-building state of leadership, the opportunist state is empowered leadership utilized effectively by the greatest leaders in the world. You may recognize such leaders in your work environments as those who display sound judgment and the ability to create their own level of success, combined with inspiring others to take on roles of greater success.

The opportunist state is the gateway to becoming the Inspired Authentic Leader. This leadership state demonstrates a vision of greatness and a desire to gain access to the creator and mastery states of leadership success. Leaders who exhibit the opportunist state are very calm, confident and authentic, capable of creating their own success while motivating and inspiring others. They are deeply accepting of others and view each situation as an opportunity instead of a challenge. They have the keen ability to make each experience a work of art through their own inspiration, creativity and wisdom.

They lead from a place of solutions rather than viewing challenges as a problem, and they show a sense of comfort in their ability to step into the unknown to experience new opportunities. Leaders in an opportunist state embrace self-realization in their expanded awareness and focus on their strengths to create success regardless of the situation that presents itself. You will recognize this leader as someone in your workplace who stands out. They will inspire you, as you feel a certain connection to them, though you may not know why. They often show the ability to bypass the needs of the ego and embrace more of a global perspective as an opportunity to create, thrive and embrace success. In this state, leaders need to tap into the compassionate heart energy of the cheerleader state, add the skillful mind energy of the opportunist state, and create the combination of leadership skills needed to be a model leader with a vision of greatness. Such a vision supports unlimited success for leaders, coworkers and teams, as well as the corporations and clients they serve.

The opportunist leadership state offers the path to self-mastery, and it is a doorway to becoming an Inspired Authentic Leader.

It is a leadership presence that has the expanded awareness necessary to access other leadership states, including the creator and mastery states of leadership success.

■ *Creator State*

The next success-building state of leadership to review is the creator state. Leaders who lead from a creator state are powerful yet humble; they know their level of excellence and continue to focus on growing and learning. The creator state is the home of visionaries and genius-mind attributes that show the ability to positively impact others around them in a profound way. They show a keen ability to access their intuition and experience a sense of fearlessness and oneness with everyone they meet.

Leaders at this state have shown their ability to move well beyond the barriers shown in lower states of leadership such as the victim and dominance states. They are highly creative with a sense of joy, wisdom and a keen focus on oneness. There is a deep level of self-respect and respect for all other leaders they encounter. This is a place of powerful partnerships where they respect and value each person for their unique gifts and strengths.

Leaders who embrace the creator state of leadership use their ability to connect with others without judgment. They have a presence that is inspiring, authentic and frequently attracts a large team around them to combine their talents and successes.

You may notice this leader in your workplace as someone who is often asked to function as a mentor or role model. They have shown leadership success that far exceeds traditional roles of success. You will notice them for their character qualities of peacefulness, supreme intuitive wisdom, a commitment to unity and oneness between all people and projects, and a greater sense of joy and awareness. The visual that comes to mind is a butterfly, transformed from a caterpillar to be the most exquisite being imaginable. A butterfly evokes ideals of beauty, wisdom, and profound awareness of their purpose and presence inside and outside their leadership roles.

One of the primary challenges for this leader is to stay grounded and in touch with others at all states of leadership. They must maintain their ability to communicate with individuals who are struggling in the lower states of leadership while holding a connection to the higher states of leadership success. The experience of the creator state is deeply fulfilling and fueled with gratitude and a love for life. Sometimes, it might be easy to get distracted in the perspective of this experience of leadership and lose a connection to the people who live in other states of leadership.

Do you relate to the qualities and characteristics of this leadership state? Can you identify an experience when you've shown some of these leadership traits and felt the flow and ease that these traits offer? Do you know someone in your office or career who stands out in your memory as showing some of these qualities? Reflect on a few of these questions to discover how you experience the energetic presence of this state. As you visualize people you have known who have shown some of these qualities, notice how the thought of that person makes you feel. Did you find a sense of peace within or did you feel increased creativity, inspiration or comfort? Maybe you remember someone you respect who makes it enjoyable to be in their presence.

Organizations, teams, projects, and other sources of collective leaders can also take on the role of the creator state and all other leadership success states. When this occurs, you often notice high levels of employee retention, employee satisfaction statistics soar, and a sense of unity exists among the employees working there. The creator state holds the power of both potential and empowerment that you can access, even if it's for short intervals in the work day.

Mastery State

The highest leadership state is the mastery state, a powerful and empowering success-building state of leadership. It is a place of access and connection to your authentic being more than a destination or a place of arrival. There are no leaders who live at the mastery state for extended periods of time. Leaders at some stages of their career have access to the mastery state and experience the magnificence it provides. The mastery state is the home of pure potential and maximized success.

If you can envision the most powerful and impactful success imaginable, the mastery state would live there. This is a place of your ideal vision of success. The mastery state is a placeholder for your vision of greatness, an experience of leadership that inspires you and leads you forward into a never-ending journey of greatness. It is not a final destination; it is the actual reason for the journey that continues to evolve and expand. There is no end to the potential in your ability to experience limitless success.

The mastery state of leadership can be compared to a flower that continues to grow and bloom, reaching for the sunlight in its evolution to becoming a masterful beauty filled with magnificence—perhaps an iris, rose, lily or sunflower. Each leader has something to aspire to, a vision that is unique to each person.

The mastery state of leadership success is a presence that directs your focus on being the absolute best leader you can envision and demonstrates leadership experience that is free from barriers to success. Leaders who experience this state of mastery, even for a short duration, will experience a deep sense of inner peace, freedom, ease and flow. There will be no judgment, only unconditional love and a deeper sense of connection to your authenticity and true nature. There is a feeling of freedom from limiting beliefs, inner critics, assumptions, interpretations and any other self-created barrier that stands in the way of success.

The mastery state is your home for your greatest success and the experience of your ideal vision of how success is defined for you.

Personal Experience with the Mastery State

Delving deeper into the lessons of my personal experience with the mastery state of leadership success, this occurred after a large "must-win" proposal that I managed for a large Fortune 100 corporation. My team included highly skilled engineers, staff members, executives, and proposal team managers brought together to win a $102 million-dollar contract. The contract was up for competitive bids with many companies ready and eager to win. The customer was looking for new innovations along with the best technical solutions, top talent and impressive price strategies.

I often reflect upon the hardships and challenges that arose during the many months of preparing a winning solution that surpassed the most talented competitors in the market. I now recognize the many situations in which the energy, character qualities and impact of all seven states of leadership success were experienced personally and collectively with each leader on our large, amazing team.

There were many times when we felt the energy of the victim leadership state, lacking resources, time or focus required to create such a grand solution. There were also periods of struggle and frustration when our hard work was altered by the executives at the top to limit the pricing or technical solutions. We sometimes felt frustrated, limited and increasingly stressed from some of the senior executive management's recommendations. There were moments of contemplation when we felt like submitting a status quo proposal and settling for a solution that responded "yes" to all the "shall" statements and "must have" requests. The times we considered taking the easy way blended with moments of gratitude and a deep desire to ensure that the solution we crafted would, in fact, help the customer achieve their mission success.

This situation demonstrates the cheerleader state, which presented itself as compassion and commitment to our customer and as the proposal team members' support for each other. As time continued to unfold, day after day, I noticed that the energy of the team was shifting into a new creative and productive type of energy. In this long journey, we overcame the frustrations of working long hours, nights and weekends, often feeling overwhelmed and stressed by the task ahead, and we became focused, committed, and aligned with the potential solutions that lived within the opportunist state of leadership success.

Our team was then aligned, focused, inspired and determined to remove all distractions. We asked the questions, "What if?" and "Why not?" And we explored the question, "How can we build upon the collective expertise of each member of our team?"

This place of inquiry filled our team with a sense of unity and oneness that demonstrated the energy of the creator leadership success state. Our experience of the creator leadership success state generated excitement and helped us identify innovative solutions. Once we started to explore, listen, and lean in to the potential of technology and innovation, this awareness moved our conversations from focusing on a status quo solution to a solution that was strategic and aligned with the customer's needs.

In time, we became more entrenched in the expression of our ideas, concepts and technical awareness, releasing all attachment to the idea of spending hours working on an effort that might not receive the winning bid. Our team had become a team of talented contributors all working together seamlessly with a combined focus and the energy of excellence as the guiding principle.

Collectively, we experienced the mastery leadership state of success, realizing the power of people and potential to experience a level of greatness that far surpassed the unknown outcome of the winning bid. As we completed the proposal, and edited, copied and bound it for customer delivery, there was a true sense of pride and team accomplishment combined with a willingness to release the final product without attachment to the outcome. Collectively, we experienced a profound state of mastery, having shown the courage to overcome the many challenges of the lower states of leadership success. We recognized each person as a member of an integral team that was part of something greater, with a sense of flow, ease, and a state of being that was truly special.

As the team dismantled and went back to routine tasks as leadership professionals, the collective bond continued to be alive with emotion and appreciation for one another. This is an example of the energy that truly contributes to great success, as exemplified in this challenging and rewarding proposal experience.

After a few months of deliberation and evaluation, the customer selected our proposal as the winning bid, based upon assessment of the best technical solution, top talent and sound pricing strategies. They awarded our team the $102 million-dollar six-year contract that was selected out of a large pool of highly competitive corporations, all eager to take ownership of this new opportunity. This was an excellent experience of living and leading through each of the seven states of leadership success. It is an experience I will never forget and often revisit in conversations with many of the team members who contributed to our win.

It is important to note that the mastery state represents the highest state of leadership success. It is the optimized and maximized experience of success. Leaders who have the skills and ability to experience the mastery state of leadership success also have the awareness and skills to access all the other six states of leadership success as desired. They have the awareness and skills needed to harness the energy and create the desired impact that each leadership state offers. Leaders at the mastery state have become masterful with the profound opportunity and impact of each state. They have skills to master the energy of each state of success to build connections, communicate, and create their desired experience of success, which promotes peace, fulfillment, and internal and external harmony.

Becoming an Inspired Authentic Leader, one that shows a state of self-mastery and increased levels of success is a master at managing their leadership states. They understand the impact of the success-blocking leadership states and how to maintain their energy to recognize if they drop into one of these experiences. Leaders in this state have the tools, skills, and awareness they need to transform their focus into a more powerful, success-oriented leadership state. Understanding the value and the potential of each of the seven leadership success states is key to becoming an Inspired Authentic Leader, a true state of self-mastery. It is mastery built upon the ability to optimize energetic presence to create maximized success.

Bringing it All Together

The self-management section puts your energy into action and promotes an awareness for creating increased levels of leadership success. It builds upon the seven states of leadership success detailed in the self-leadership section. Self-management uncovers who you are being in each moment and how your success is impacted by the leadership success state and quality of energy being used.

The focus of self-management was on "who you are being" as a leader and how that awareness aligns with one of the seven leadership success states. You built upon the awareness of energy as either success-building energy that creates success or success-blocking energy that obstructs success.

You expanded your awareness by considering the creative potential in the Success Creator Model, which defined beliefs as the generator that determines success. You revisited the ideal-vision-of-success statement that was defined in the self-leadership section and combined this vision with one or more of the seven leadership success states to identify the quality and character of energy required to experience your vision of success. You explored the gap of opportunity, using the Success Barometer to reveal your current leadership success state compared to your desired leadership success state. This exploration helps close the gap between your current experience of success and your desired experience of success.

In addition, you embraced the power of pause and its importance for creating a pause between situations and your response to the situation, versus allowing a triggered reaction to burst from a place of crisis and drama. You uncovered each of the four energy busters that live at the root of all your challenges, struggles, and limited experiences of success.

The awareness, insights and new perspectives discovered in this section are transformational. As Inspired Authentic Leaders, you shift your perspective from experiences of traditional leadership success to authentic leadership success, increasing personal fulfillment and a renewed sense of freedom and flow.

Key Takeaways:

- Who am I being in each moment?

- What state of leadership success and qualities do I use to create success?

- Am I using my energy to create success or block success?

- Do I respond to situations or do I react to them?

- Which of the four energy busters are limiting my success?

- Do I lead from a traditional role of leadership success or an authentic role of leadership success?

You have made a lot of progress on your journey from self-leadership to self-management, and your ability to utilize your energy and awareness to increase success. Now continue to expand your awareness in the next section and take the next step to become strong self-mastery leaders. Then, you will be prepared to catapult your success experience with unlimited potential.

Section Four...

Self-Mastery

14. The Power of Self-Mastery

Do you remember a time over the course of your life or career when you experienced yourself performing at the top of your game?

Can you recall an experience when you might have felt outside yourself, functioning at a level well beyond your routine mode of operation?

As you reflect upon this situation, you may remember a sense of ease and flow associated with your experience and perhaps felt surprised or even in shock.

This sense of ease and flow might have surfaced during or after you completed an important presentation, a speech in front of a large audience or related to any situation in which you excelled. Most likely, this experience created a success-oriented impact that was measurable and meaningful. Remember how great that experience felt? How happy, excited and inspired were you?

It's interesting that you can often align your success potential to function at a supreme state of success without even realizing what you did.

This is the experience of self-mastery, when you are in partnership with the energy of the moment and use your resources to perform with a sense of ease and increased levels of freedom, flow and fulfillment. Would you agree that having strong self-mastery skills and becoming the Inspired Authentic Leader provides the capacity to experience these increased levels of performance and success-oriented experiences? Might this be the game changer you've been seeking?

I hope you're excited because this is the goal of working together and exploring self-mastery.

Self-masters are highly skilled at maximizing their energy in the moment to create their desired vision of success. They have the increased ability to free themselves of past experiences and future desires to partner with the potential of the moment. That ability ensures maximized success. They live and lead in the present moment, using their aligned energy toward fulfilling the needs of the moment and mastering their skills of presence and performance during each potential to experience success.

The experience of self-mastery helps you perform without over-thinking, without worry, hesitation or fear. Self-mastery puts you into the flow of potential and places you at the cornerstone of true inner peace. Your connection to inner wisdom and an experience of freedom becomes deeply fulfilling. Instead of focusing on leadership, you will become a leader who reflects a profound state of being, with an expression of you as your best self that is unlike anything you've experienced before. **Your ability to focus on the experience in the moment is a skill you will cherish for a lifetime.**

Most people confuse their success goals with their primary goals. They believe what they are searching for is the outcome itself, when in fact, the success goal is the feeling that lives beneath the primary goal. That feeling may be satisfaction, inner peace, excitement, passion, joy, accomplishment or an emotion that only occurs once they achieve the goal.

Today's seasoned leaders have been trained to focus on the tangible aspects of leadership, the external goals, deadlines and outcomes that keep them in the win column and support the many roles in which they excel. The one thing that is often missing in a leader's ability to create and experience success is how to perform consistently at their best. How to optimize and maximize their success so they experience both the inner and outer qualities, and the tangible and intangible rewards of authentic success.

They discover this desire to experience authentic success in the depths of self-mastery. This is an invitation to leaders from all walks of life to embrace a state of self-mastery as a leadership journey and an opportunity to experience the greatness that drives them forward to optimal states of success.

Self-mastery is a state of "being" that focuses on living and leading in the present moment, letting go of the past or future and focusing on the opportunity in the moment.

Instead of performing or leading, you actually become your performance, a mastery experience that becomes a part of you and expresses your greatest potential.

> *"Self-Knowledge is the Stepping Stone to Self-Mastery"*
> -Robin Sharma

Self-mastery leadership is best explained by recalling the story of the "Black Belt." The Sensei asked the student each year for three continuous years why he should earn the black belt.

The first two years the student responded that he should earn the black belt because it marked an end to his journey and awarded him for his great effort. Each year, the Sensei was displeased with the student's awareness, and the student was told to return in one year. Not until the third year when the student responded, "The Black Belt represents not the end, but the beginning, the start of a never-ending journey of discipline, work and the pursuit of an ever-higher standard." The Sensei was satisfied with the student's response and knew he was indeed ready to receive the honor of the black belt.

In this story, the student evolved to a deeper understanding of the meaning of the black belt. He had transformed his awareness from an achievement of completion to a renewed mark of a new beginning. Instead of an award, the black belt signified his depth in awareness and willingness to adhere to a state of being aligned with a state of mastery. It was this renewed thinking and commitment to a way of being that awarded him the black belt.

The story illustrates the essence of the self-mastery leadership success state that we are exploring and uncovering throughout each chapter of this book. Self-mastery is a vision of being exceptional, identifying the ideal vision of success and aligning that vision with a renewed state of being. This new state of being promotes opportunities to learn, grow, experience, and express your awareness. These are key aspects to the experience and expression of self-mastery.

Self-mastery leadership starts with a vision of your desired experience and a realization that whatever you desire is already a part of you waiting to be expressed. Otherwise, why would you feel a connection to it? Your ability to connect with and experience this innermost state of your desired "being" lives within a practice to release judgment and defined outcomes about how to experience it. You must be willing to remain open to new perspectives, so you can experience each moment fully and allow it to express itself through you without attachment. Once you partner with the awareness that your desires are within you and identify the evidence that they exist, your opportunities for creating and experiencing your desired success goals become limitless.

Personally, I take great comfort in knowing each of you has the self-mastery skills you desire within you and available to use each moment. Although the goal in this book is to increase your awareness and connection with self-mastery, essentially you already have within you everything you could ever desire. The difference is your acceptance of this awareness and your ability to embrace it in each moment.

Becoming a strong self-master is an ongoing journey, a never-ending process that continues to unfold like a small fern growing in a meadow. As you visualize this young fern starting its journey toward the sunlight and continuing its growth into maturity, note that the fern does not waste energy worrying if it will reach its full potential. It has a willingness to experience and express itself each moment trusting its own intelligence to evolve fully into its true nature.

Your journey into self-mastery requires trusting the process and relying on your own internal energy and strength to empower you to keep growing, like the fern, and reach your success goals. Self-mastery is similar to the growing fern; the journey requires a willingness to let go of the outcome, to be comfortable in the unknown and to trust that everything you need is available in each moment as it presents itself.

Masters from all walks of life agree, you cannot control the outcomes or results, you can only take ownership of how you respond to life in each moment. This is true whether you are a high-performing athlete, artist, musician, spiritual guru, philosopher, or any other role that functions from a mastery leadership state. Each moment is the key, offering you true opportunities to create success. The power to create and experience success lives in the moment. *"Who you are being"* in each moment shapes your life and defines the momentum of your success.

Your ability to create and experience success depends upon the direction of your momentum and if it's leading you toward your vision of success or away from your vision of success. In the self-mastery state, you become much more aware and aligned with the magic of the moment and the impact it has on your overall progress to either experience the emotions related to your desired success or those feelings attached to being limited or stuck in the yearning stage.

Self-mastery leadership is a willingness to practice a process of discovery and to lean into the unknown to explore the energy of questions like, *"What if?"* and *"Why not?"* It invites you to ask many difficult questions and to be open to what wants to happen in each moment. It is an opportunity to perceive each situation as an opportunity to excel and let go of the many labels you use to describe each experience. You no longer define the specifics of each outcome. When you embrace a self-mastery approach to leadership, it quiets the intellectual mind and embraces a fresh perspective that opens new possibilities and potential.

Self-mastery leadership is also a holistic approach, focused on the balance between intrinsic and extrinsic awareness and on the leadership presence that exists while doing the necessary tasks. The left brain of logic is combined with the right brain of creativity, and the intangible qualities are infused with the tangible goals. It centers the focus upon the anabolic success-building energy, and the passion and purpose that exists within every performance and engagement. A full understanding and deep awareness of each activity is essential to create a bridge between both aspects that combine holistically to become the whole. The level of flow and balance is best understood by considering the Chinese principles of yin and yang. Both aspects of energy are necessary to complete the totality of the experience.

For example, imagine you desire to become a successful speaker, one who has the gift of confidence, engagement, charisma, and all the other qualities that a professional speaker typically demonstrates. Using this vision of you as a successful speaker, notice the qualities you believe to be the most impactful ones that contribute to a speaker's success. What would these qualities be? Confidence, clarity, comfort?

Make a list of five to seven primary qualities. As you review the list of qualities you believe are vital to becoming a successful speaker, focus in on three primary qualities. Then ask yourself, "When have I experienced this quality in my life?" Has there been a time you experienced a success using these qualities? Explore each of the three qualities to identify evidence that those qualities live within your presence and potential, as well.

Once you realize that each of these desired qualities are within your capacity for success, create an action plan for how you might include them in your daily routines. Practice each quality, role play just like a professional actor might prepare for a role in the latest hit movie being released. Experience each of these qualities until they become automatically part of your state of being. How confident are you after doing this inspired discovery exercise? You have within you the qualities, and everything you need, to create and experience your desired level of success.

When you practice this self-empowerment exercise, you will notice that the qualities you desire are already within you and awaiting to express themselves. Once you show a willingness and openness to experience and explore new opportunities, you uncover each desired quality that lives within your being state, and a new state of leadership success surfaces and opens the door to greater fulfillment. The next chapter delves deeper into the self-mastery mindset to enhance your experience of authentic leadership and limitless success.

15. Establishing a Self-Mastery Mindset

Leaders who use the power of the mastery leadership success state are curious and free of judgment. They show an open mind with no preconceived notions. They are excited about new possibilities and new experiences. Energetically, a leader with a self-mastery mindset lives in the "now." They are free from their previous experiences and past results, showing a curiosity and openness to the experience taking place in each moment. They live from a true authentic presence that is fully engaged and aligned with the energy and activity being experienced within each moment of their day. This gives them access to their power and full potential that resides in the present moment. They are free from the limitations of their thought patterns and analytical tendencies, fully aligned and engaged with their capacity to create and experience their desired success. When we lead with a self-mastery mindset, we are in a highly anabolic success-oriented state ready to experience life fully as it unfolds naturally.

Leaders skilled with a self-mastery mindset do not forget the learned skills of their professional expertise. They maintain their knowledge and wisdom obtained from all previous experiences. There are no defined experiences and perspectives on how the world should function. Rather, a leader with a self-mastery mindset recognizes new patterns, new connections and new possibilities. They invite new visions and opportunities that promote new ideas and insights aligned with limitless success.

As you reflect on the self-mastery mindset, consider another view of multi-tasking, an example that may enhance your understanding.

How often during your work day do you find yourself multi-tasking on several projects at the same time? Are you thinking, "Wait a minute, multi-tasking is a great skill for efficiency and productivity, and that's what we've learned in every time-management class we've ever taken, right?"

I can relate, with my career history as a Senior Program Manager with heavy performance and efficiency requirements. My keen ability to multi-task contributed to my team's success. However, looking closely at multi-tasking reveals more facts. Multi-tasking is about distributing your energy, breaking down the energy and directing it into multiple areas of focus. It minimizes the pure potential for a high quality, high caliber performance, product or power.

Multi-tasking divides your skills and awareness into several directions, and you may lose your ability to produce an efficient, effective outcome. Imagine a stream of light that is being directed at one group of flowers in a greenhouse instead of the light being directed at the entire room. Which light would offer the greatest potential? This example depicts the same awareness for you as leaders and working professionals. The quality of your work and success depends upon how you use your energy and toward what goal it is being directed.

In previous chapters you explored traditional leadership compared to authentic leadership, and the goal of becoming an Inspired Authentic Leader as a renewed state of self-mastery. Establishing a self-mastery mindset requires you to transform your leadership focus from traditional leadership mindsets that use your energy to multi-task and produce in large quantities to authentic leadership that maximizes your energy, directing 100 percent of your resources to produce high-quality performances and products.

Maximize Your Energetic Capacity

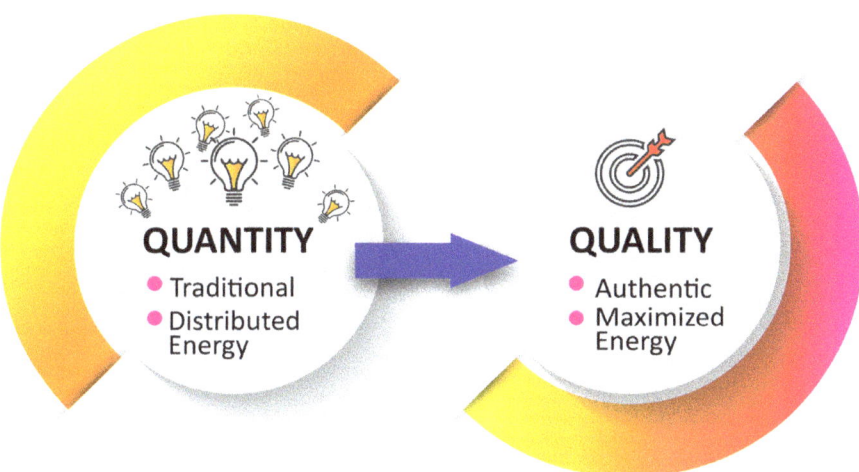

*Self-Mastery combines **quality** with **quantity** by optimizing and maximizing your energetic capacity while minimizing the time it takes to create and experience success.*

When you maximize your energy and awareness, you have the skills to create both quality and quantity at the same time.

As you increase your ability to focus solely on the task in each moment, it removes all distractions and reduces the time to complete the experience of your desires. Authentic leadership focuses on being effective and efficient, using skills that are everlasting regardless of the situation.

ENGAGING THE ENERGY OF SUCCESS

Have you ever noticed how much of your energy is diluted by the drama in each situation? I'd like to share with you a simplified model for engagement that I absolutely love. Presented by Alan Seale in his book, titled *Transformational Presence: How to Make a Difference in a Rapidly Changing World,* Alan Seale refers to the **Four Levels of Awareness and Engagement** as the "DSCO" model. DSCO is an acronym for **D**rama, **S**ituation, **C**hoice and **O**pportunity — the four levels of awareness from which we engage with our daily experiences.

The Four Levels of Engagement

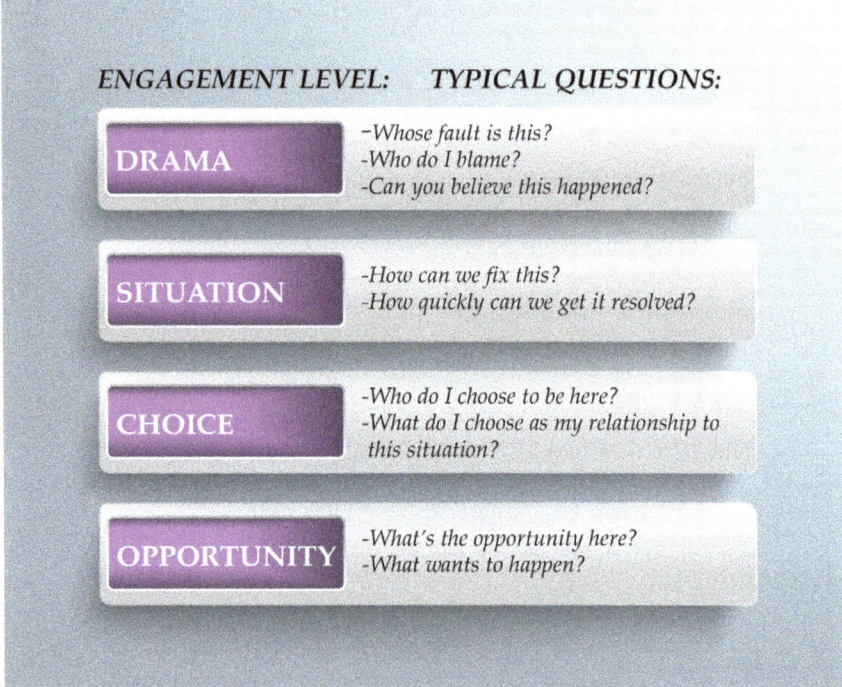

The model shown in the table above provides a structure for getting to the true nature of what is going on as quickly as possible. It expands our awareness and gives us the process we need to shift our energy into a more empowering, productive state. Let's explore each of the levels of engagement.

DRAMA
Drama lives at the surface of the situation, where the chaos begins. "He says, she says. This happened and then that happened." The drama promotes the area of distortion and heightened emotion to enhance the story. It is easy to get caught up in the energy of this state and react to what is being said. This is the story that is being revealed with all the juicy details about the perceived experience. It is easy to get into a reactive triggered response instead of choosing how you would like to respond. Even for seasoned leaders, it is not uncommon to get pulled into a drama state, especially if you have an emotional attachment to a desired outcome.

The drama level is very similar to the dominance leadership success state. Do you notice the same tendencies of blaming, creating a story, and looking to pinpoint the fault on others? Imagine a similar experience you've encountered when you got caught up in a drama level situation. How did you feel? What happened to your focus and energy? How productive, engaged, inspired, effective were you? Even leaders that lead from a place of self-mastery can sometimes drop momentarily into a drama state. However, they have the tools and awareness necessary to shift their energy into a more productive and empowering anabolic state of engagement, so they less frequently get caught up in the drama.

SITUATION

In the situation level of engagement, the true facts begin to be identified more clearly, and there is a better understanding of what actually happened instead of attaching a dramatic story to the facts. The most common question becomes, "How do we fix this?" This approach is all about damage control and getting the situation back to normal. It is a band-aid, a quick solution without recognizing what contributed to the original concern or challenge. As a result, a similar situation or challenge is likely to surface again because the underlying root of the issue was never addressed. Routinely, challenges and situations are most often addressed by identifying, "Who did what?" "Why?" and "How can we fix it?" types of queries and responses. Both the drama and situation levels of engagement relate to traditional forms of leadership responses and do not promote a success-oriented perspective that is needed for maximized success.

CHOICE

The choice level of engagement opens the door to the anabolic energy that lives at the status quo leadership success state and shows the true essence of self-leadership. It invites us to shift our awareness and perspective of each situation. At this level, we are no longer focused on fixing the problem; instead our focus centers upon "Who do we want to be in relation to this situation?" Essentially, the choice level reminds us of our "being" state and which state of leadership success needs to be evoked to respond to this challenge. Some questions that come up at this level might include, "What is my role in how this situation came to be?" "What is my role in what is happening now?" "How do I engage going forward?"

The choice level invites us to consider that although we may not change the circumstance or situation, we can at least choose who we will be within the experience. This is authentic leadership in action, a state of self-mastery I call the Inspired Authentic Leader. At this state, we take personal responsibility for how we engage with the situation, who we will be in relationship to the situation and how we will respond in the moment of the experience.

OPPORTUNITY

In the fourth level of engagement lives opportunity, which offers a doorway to creating true sustaining success. This is the home to the most profound leadership in the world, leading from a place of true self-mastery. It shares qualities of the opportunist leadership success state in that it shows the willingness to perceive all experiences as opportunities instead of problems or challenges. It bases the true success potential on our ability to ask different questions, like "What's the opportunity or potential in this situation?" and "What wants to happen here?" This is where the true success power and potential live. What might be possible if we perceive each situation as a purpose or a conduit of message and meaning? What if we viewed each situation as an indicator of awareness, a message, insight or point of concern it wants to show us, as an opportunity to recognize clearly what is not working or what wants to change or heal? There is often a direct correlation between the drama and the opportunity. The bigger the challenge the greater the opportunity. This is a wake-up call alerting you that something wants to shift or transform. It is energy in action that promotes the potential to listen and partner with it to recreate new levels of awareness and success.

We have discussed in the self-leadership and self-management sections of this book the importance of overcoming the barriers to success by minimizing the catabolic energy and partnering with the anabolic leadership success states. The same concepts apply to the four levels of awareness and engagement models.

What if, instead of responding to a situation or challenge through the eyes of the drama and situation levels of engagement, you respond with the energy of the choice and opportunity levels of engagement? Instead of being triggered by the catabolic levels of the drama and situation levels, you focus your attention on experiencing the anabolic potential of the choice and opportunity levels where freedom, flow and fulfillment live. How might this minimize your stress, distraction, and limited success while maximizing your fulfillment, focus and flow of success? Does this awareness resonate with you?

Another helpful tip in using this model is to use the pause concept discussed in the self-management section. In the middle of the four levels of engagement, there is room to add a pause to create a space and a renewed awareness. When you apply the practice of pause between the drama/situation and the choice/opportunity levels, this creates time and space for increased awareness and clarity of choice.

If you find yourself in a triggered state identifying with either the drama or situation experience, practice the pause technique, focusing on the breath. Notice the breath moving slowly in and out of each nostril. Check in with the sensations of your body, noticing what you are feeling and your overall physical state. Is your heart beating rapidly or slowly? Just notice. This practice of pause will

give you the space and time you need to reconnect with your self-leadership skills and help you transform your attention to the choice and opportunity types of engagement.

When we live in a drama or situation experience, life is about struggle and problem solving. We give away our power and place the focus on something outside ourselves, outside our control, which keeps us feeling stuck, limited and less empowered. When we move to the choice and opportunity levels of engagement, we take back our power. We consciously choose who we will be and how we will respond to each situation. This simple shift in perspective puts us in an empowered instead of a disempowered state. The energy of the choice and opportunity levels helps us to break free from the struggle of the catabolic experience and create a new anabolic experience that sustains success.

Before we end our discussion on the DSCO model or the Four Levels of Awareness and Engagement, I'd like to emphasize the most important aspect of this transformational model. If you are a person on the fast track who likes to identify one point of emphasis, then this is for you. Asking "What wants to happen?" has been one of the most life-changing questions I've ever experienced. Essentially, asking that question supports your ability to sense the energy beneath the situation, beneath the words being spoken or the actions being shown.

This is a transformational tool that has the potential to expand your awareness and enhance your experience of increased success. When you consider the opportunity of the moment, instead of reacting or putting out fires and quickly moving to the next crisis of the day, you expand your potential for success. You lead from a place of creativity, partnering with the unknown to show a willingness and openness for new insight, wisdom and limitless potential.

Living and leading from the choice and opportunity levels requires courage, authenticity, and a desire to move beyond traditional roles of leadership into new levels of authentic leadership. This shift creates increased experiences of success. This renewed leadership requires focus, discipline, and the boldness to step beyond drama to identify the opportunity rather than just solve the problem. It starts with being driven enough to choose who you will be, to decide what relationship you will have with each circumstance you encounter, and a commitment to a dedicated practice that includes asking the questions, "What wants to happen? What's the opportunity here?" These are the pivotal questions that contribute to increased levels of success.

THE COIN THEORY OF LEADERSHIP SUCCESS

As I practiced and used the Four Levels of Awareness and Engagement over the years, I developed a simple system for ensuring that I maintain my focus on the choice and opportunity states of success. I call this system the Coin Theory of Leadership Success. Imagine having a large gold coin that has tremendous value. On one side of the coin are the words *Drama* and *Situation*, and on the opposite side of the coin are the words *Choice* and *Opportunity*. Sometimes, I envision the words describing a problem on one side of the coin and a solution to the problem on the other side of the coin.

Each side of the coin represents the potential of choice or intention for being explored and expressed. To use this awareness, consider the next time you experience a less-than-desirable situation filled with the energy of drama and situation, you consider both sides of the coin's potential. Note the transformation that exists in the awareness of both the opportunity and the solution within each situation. There is never a situation that doesn't include an opportunity or potential solution within it. The outcome of your success will depend upon which side of the coin you use to experience and create success. Your ability to make a conscious decision to turn the coin to the side where choice and opportunity live will empower you to experience increased levels of success by finding the solution within the situation.

If you choose to focus on the side of the coin where drama and situation live, your success will be limited and unproductive because your energy will be drained, and your focus will be distracted by the fabricated stories that exist in these two perspectives. The coin theory provides a visual aid to help you remember the power of your perceptions and your ability to shift your perspectives and consider multiple ways to view any experience. Turn the coin to view a new empowering perspective. This action not only shifts the energy but expands your awareness on the duality that lives between the problem and its solution.

The Art of Self-Mastery

As an Inspired Authentic Leader who is focused on the state of self-mastery, you have the innate ability to see opportunity everywhere and create success automatically.

You have an increased ability to show a state of mastery that is a learned skill and a deepened awareness that fuels passion and propels you forward to unlimited success. Becoming the energetic embodiment of the Inspired Authentic Leader transforms your leadership potential from the limitations of traditional roles of leadership and opens the door to increased opportunities to experience success.

This renewed potential includes the opportunity to transform the workplace from a state of command and control to a setting for co-creation. Such a workplace provides artistry, affording a renewed ability to create and craft your life's work as your own masterpiece of success that is filled with clarity, connection and contribution. This is the new energy and spirit that mastering the skills of self-mastery brings to workplace success. This is the vision of the future, the opportunity to feed your spirit and nurture your soul with the insights and experiences you so deeply desire. This is the energy of the Inspired Authentic Leader: alive, vibrant and vividly visible in every workplace across the continent and beyond. The impact of this energy can enliven every workplace professional with the inspiration and an invitation to go beyond, to be exceptional and eager to excel.

As you uncover the potential for self-mastery and its ability to transform the workplace to be one of artistry, impact, and fueled by the energy of success, it's the perfect opportunity to tap into the self-mastery skills of the creative process.

Artists are masters at demonstrating the creative process. They use their mastery skills to chip away the unformed to reveal the new, to transform each art form into a renewed state, to release the illusion of the unknown and explore the true beauty of its potential.

Artists are not drawing, painting, or composing at random. They first have a clear vision of what they want to create and use their power to connect energetically with the vision of their desired success. They show the ability to sense the energy behind their vision of desire and use their sensory skills to connect with the overall experience. This combined energetic experience integrates the use of their artistic skills, processes, and passion to bring this vision into existence — to make the vision real. As this process unfolds, they become free from the fear of what others may think, and they are released from any worries about getting it right. They invite their passion and skills to guide the production of their art.

Inspired Authentic Leaders are the artists of their own visions for success. They tap into their highest levels of anabolic thinking to create a desired vision for themselves and others. They experience this vision through each of their senses, which ignites their passion and aligns their potential for increased success. Not only do they master their own presence and state of being; they also identify the strengths and talents of their team members to bring about the most profound results. Each moment provides a unique opportunity for the artist to partner with the potential of the moment, to chip away at the illusions of the conditioned mind and to transform their energy and focus to experiencing the essence of their true potential.

As leaders, you are each empowered with the energy of success, with the desire for greatness and the ability to create on a magnitude that far exceeds your current level of awareness.

As you entertain the potential that exists to transform the workplace to be one of mastery, artistry and impact, into an experience that unleashes your greatest ideas and innovations, you become deeply fulfilled. Can you imagine a workplace that is filled with the energy of creativity, innovation, mastery and profound impact? How does this look and feel to you? Do you believe it would transform the workplace and promote higher levels of personal fulfillment, increased productivity, greater performance and overall combined success? What might the impact be to your health and well-being if you routinely embodied the energy of the artist in your work day?

To become one with the task at hand, regardless if you are focused on writing a proposal, staying fully present in the moment while talking to a coworker and listening on all levels for communications shared or harnessing your success energy while preparing a powerful, fully engaged presentation.

There are limitless opportunities to become the master of your work life. From large, highly visible, high-impact tasks to other insignificant tasks, you can excel beyond your current levels of success. When you become skilled in your awareness of the opportunity in each moment, letting go of your thoughts and surrendering to become still, present, focused and engaged in the full potential of each moment, imagine what might be possible.

There are no attachments or distractions in the now. Attachments limit your potential. When you learn to release your attachment to a defined outcome, you surrender, allowing the experience of the present moment to carry you forward to limitless success. This is the experience of self-mastery and the way of the Inspired Authentic Leader.

The next chapter details six game-changing energetic success factors.

16. Six Game-Changing Factors that Determine Your Success

What influences your success?

Regardless of how well trained or seasoned a leader you may be, various inner and outer aspects can impact you, building or blocking your success. These influences are the six dimensions to success that I refer to as the Energetic Success Factors. By understanding these success factors and knowing how to apply them, you have a huge advantage as a leader who creates consistent and effective experiences and maximizes success.

Self-mastery is about maximizing your energy, focus and awareness in such a way that you use 100 percent of your true potential to create success. If a situation distracts you, you're unable to focus and your success is limited. Just like a tire on an automobile that has a small leak, losing the vital air needed to perform optimally, your energy is leaking and reduced to a non-optimal condition.

To maintain a high volume of success building potential, you are encouraged to learn how to maximize each of the six energetic success factors that include emotional, mental, physical, spiritual, social and environmental factors. You need to consider the impact of each energetic success factor as an individual contributor to a combined state of success. Just like each spoke of a wheel is necessary to ensure the overall functionality of the wheel that rolls properly. The energetic success factors are holistic, each contributing to the whole "integrated" potential to create and experience success. Each factor supports and compliments the others to form a synergistic momentum to help you manage and master the energetic capacity for maximized success.

The energetic success factor that most impacts success varies from person to person, and sometimes, from situation to situation. Anytime you are not experiencing the success you desire, something is blocking and limiting your success. Most often it is an impact from one of the six energetic factors that is preventing you from reaching your desired level of success.

Exploring the six energetic success factors will bring to light some of the ways they show up within the many aspects of your work life. In a routine day, you likely experience each one of them collectively and independently. The question to consider is, how are these factors affecting your success? Are they success-building and working for you to create success or are they success-blocking, working against you to limit your success? The goal is to overcome the internal and external blocks that prevent you from experiencing your ideal vision of maximized success.

Exploring the Six Energetic Success Factors

The Emotional Success Factor

Emotions allow you to feel and experience life. They provide the texture, patterns and uniqueness to each experience and have the potential to transform your energy from a place of excitement and inspiration to frustration and feeling unhappy. Emotions are energy in motion, they have the potential to lift or lower your energetic capacity to experience success. Imagine completing a high-visibility assignment that took several months to complete. Each day you worked tirelessly to put together a stellar product. When it was completed, you received a presidential award and recognition for the quality of your solution only to discover that you have no emotion or feelings of sensations to describe this experience. Stop for a moment to consider the quality of your life without emotions. It's a little daunting. Emotions add color and volume to each area of our life.

You experience the world not only through your mind and the way you perceive and think about situations, but also through your ability to feel, sense and create a resonance with each experience. Emotions drive many of your decisions and actions; they build energy and add to the fuel of success or block energy, decreasing your success.

Emotions provide you with a strong gauge of success. You have the ability to monitor your current energetic potential and detect the quality of your energy and determine if it is supporting you in creating success or limiting your success. As an Inspired Authentic Leader, it is essential to remain cognizant of your current state of energy and the emotional qualities that are being used to create and sustain your success potential.

Most people try to avoid what feels bad instead of listening to the emotions that live just beneath the surface of each situation. You can bring those emotions to the surface simply by increasing your awareness and ability to pause, listening and exploring the following questions.

- o "What wants to happen here?"

- o "What is this emotion trying to tell me?"

- o "What is the opportunity?"

Each question provides support and gets to the root of the emotion, instead of simply covering it up so it continues to limit your success.

THE EMOTIONAL FACTOR - SENSING THE ENERGY OF SUCCESS

What impact do you believe emotions have on your success?

Your ability to focus inward and sense the pulse of your feelings offers support for detecting the potential of your success. When you notice that you are not experiencing your desired experience, you can turn your own internal detector on to sense the condition of each emotional response.

Begin by quieting the mind and imagine that you are stepping into a large scanner that has the technology required to scan each sensation that is taking place in your body. This scanner would encounter the organs functioning, the sensations of brain activity, the blood flowing throughout your body and similar responses. As you continue to scan your body, notice how the scanner realizes each emotion, the label you've assigned to a feeling, sensation or energy in motion. Just notice and capture your emotional responses.

To deepen your awareness, ask yourself two questions:

- "What am I feeling?"

- "How am I feeling?"

Notice the difference it makes when you reposition the question to begin with "what" versus "how." Beginning the question with "what" provides greater insight and awareness. When you begin the question with "how" the inquiry invites a judgment and assessment of the situation being experienced.

As you notice your emotional responses that surface because of the "what" versus "how" questions, take a step further and ask yourself, "If I am feeling these emotions, what was I thinking to create these emotions?" Notice the primary emotions that are coming up for you and how they associate to one of the seven leadership success states. Are you experiencing the fear, anxiety and struggle inherent in the victim success state? Do you feel the anger, resentment, blame and greed associated with the dominance success state or the reconciliation based on the desire for security and safety in the status quo success state? Do you feel the emotions of gratitude, love, compassion and service of the cheerleader success state?

You may also experience emotions that represent the higher states of leadership success. Do you feel the calmness, confidence and a sense of authenticity that indicates emotions of the opportunist success state? The creator success state provides emotions described as oneness, fearlessness and a joyful presence.

The mastery success state embodies feelings of passion, freedom, flow and fulfillment. Your ability to connect with and identify your emotions offers you an indicator of the quality of your success energy. As you begin to understand your emotions and the thoughts and beliefs that are driving each sensation, you become empowered with the ability to create your own pathway to success.

Your emotions create your interpretation of a situation that generates physical feelings or sensations. Emotions are a perfect method of awareness to help you determine which state of leadership success resonates with you. As you use emotional awareness to become the Inspired Authentic Leader, consider how emotions function as an advocate for increased success in each of the three elements of leadership success.

- **Self-Leadership** — You experience increased awareness of the impact of your emotions and take ownership over them.

- **Self-Management** — Emotions by choice, your ability to manage your emotions and understand the quality and impact they have on each situation. As you become co-creators with your emotions, you optimize your success potential.

- **Self-Mastery** — You develop a keen awareness of the emotional energy that exists in each moment, and you master the ability to partner with success-building emotions to generate optimal success rather than success-blocking emotions that limit success.

Emotions enhance your belief systems and what you have determined to be true. They are energetic power generators that give strength to success or hamper your ability to create success. The capacity to express your emotions in a way that effectively communicates your authentic truth is an essential element to becoming an Inspired Authentic Leader with a self-mastery mindset. Increasing your skills to express and control your emotions puts you in the power seat of success. You have the option to choose how you will respond instead of reacting to each situation. You determine where you will direct your energy and attention with the full creative potential to transform your energetic responses to become more profound, aligned, and robust to maximize your daily success.

Inspired Discovery Exercise:
As you continue to expand your awareness and connection in working with your emotions, create a daily practice for assessing your emotions at various times to notice your emotional state and ask the following questions.

- "What am I feeling?"

- What is this feeling telling me about how I'm interpreting a situation?"

- "How would I like to respond to this situation?"

- "What, if any, energetic shifts in emotions need to happen?"

Self-Mastery Insight:

It is important to understand how to assess your emotions and be able to shift them in the moment by incorporating the practice of asking yourself, "Is this emotion success-blocking or success-building?" Once you detect that you are in a success-blocking state and you need to shift the energy around the emotional experience, consider a few of the following ideas:

- Movement- Go for a brisk walk, run, or engage in some type of exercise to shift your emotional state
- Experience the energy by rubbing your hands together to shift the energy
- Laughter
- Meditate to quiet the mind
- Spend time in nature, observing and reconnecting
- View images of a place where you feel inspired and love being a part of it
- Listen to music that evokes the feelings you desire to experience
- Tune into your breathing and allow your energy to become focused and realigned
- Read inspiring quotes
- Talk to a friend who is inspiring and empowering
- Smile or practice expressions that embody the desired state
- Watch a funny movie or practice sharing a joke with others

These are just a few energy-shifting suggestions; you are invited to choose whatever path to realignment resonates with you. The important aspect to remember is to shift your energy and your state of being to a more productive, energetic success-building state.

Maximizing Your Emotional Factor to Increase Success—
When you detect the emotions that work best for you and begin to experience the success you desire, you can use this awareness to proactively generate the emotions that fuel you and keep you functioning in an optimal success-oriented state.

THE MENTAL SUCCESS FACTOR

How does the mental factor impact your success? The mental factor includes your thoughts, how your brain processes those thoughts and the impact your thoughts have on your ability to create success. It is fundamental to your capacity to be present, alert, focused and clear, so you can harness your mental power to make smart decisions, create innovative ideas and take inspired action. One of the primary aspects of the mental factor is your ability to focus and direct your energy toward the goals of your desired success. Focus is the energy you direct toward the object or situation, maximizing its potential.

Imagine using a magnifying glass to focus on a specific area on a large world map. Visualize it quickly zooming in on the chosen location in a small geographic area that is part of a vast region. As you look through the magnifying glass, you can easily focus on the pinpointed view of the area you need to see more clearly. The vast surroundings become a blurred background to the part you need to examine for greater detail. This is the same for your success generating potential. Once you focus your energy and attention on a specific outcome or goal, you optimize and maximize potential for increased success compared to other goals and desires that are outside your chosen focal point. Your laser focus on the task at hand generates energy, empowering you and the object of your focus.

Inspired Discovery Exercise:

Practice experimenting with your focus by identifying 30-minute segments throughout your day to direct your attention and energy for a specific task. You will need to remove all other distractions, close email, silence phone, close your office door and stop any other activities that could prevent you from focusing your energy fully for the 30-minute segment. You can start with one to two segments per day and increase them as desired. At the end of this experiment, notice how much you accomplished. Did you become engaged more deeply with your focused area?

When individuals focus more intently, they often recall feeling as if they were in a zone with a sense of flow and ease, an experience that is aligned with a mastery state. As you continue to experiment with this method, compare your focused experience with a non-focused experience and note how you felt during each. Notice your productivity levels in each state. How engaged were you? Did you experience success-building energy or success-blocking energy?

Removing the Energy of Clutter

Just as important as directing your focus and removing distractions is considering how clutter is getting in the way of your success. The mental clutter of too many thoughts racing through your head or too many tasks going on at the same time can stress your mental resources. Observe the physical clutter in your office or workspace and notice if it creates a visual weight. It may be helpful to reorganize the space to have less clutter and more flow.

There are many forms of clutter that require the practice of clearing to optimize and maximize your mental success. Clearing the space includes your ability to center yourself when you notice that you are feeling distracted, overwhelmed, and exerting too much energy. Having a daily practice for removing the clutter in all forms with a routine that promotes a feeling of being grounded will bring your attention back to a place of focus and power. This practice is deeply rewarding and impactful.

Recommended mind-clearing activities include meditation, which is beneficial for clearing your mind, getting back into a centered, grounded mindset and helping you to feel empowered and aligned with your core being. Yoga is another way to support deeper levels of insight and awareness. In the yoga tradition, a practice called a drishti, uses the gaze to focus solely on one point of awareness. By targeting your gaze toward an object, you anchor your mind, preventing the drifting back and forth that characterizes much mental activity over the day. With your gaze and mind completely focused on one object, you sharpen your mental skills.

Access to Creativity and Inspiration

Another mental success factor is your ability to access your creative ideas and tap into your intuition; that capability is also a critical component of leadership success. To review, creativity and intuition live in the creator and mastery leadership success states, and you can enhance and access them more frequently with practice. How often do you use creativity and intuition in your current leadership role? On a scale of one to ten, with one being the lowest value, what number would you use to rate the importance of creativity and intuition as it pertains to self-mastery and workplace success?

As you transform your perception of the workplace experience and expand your thinking to the possibility of the workplace as an innovative, creative activity that crafts your life's work in a meaningful and masterful way, you become more aware of creative sparks and intuitive insights that propel you beyond traditional experiences of success. Your ability to be creative, unique and expressive showcases your authenticity and promotes a deeper level of personal satisfaction and fulfillment.

Mental stimulation is a key element of success that ensures you experience periods of activity that challenge and energize your mental capacity combined with experiences that allow you to work in an effortless, flow state. Both aspects of mental stimulation are vital to maintaining a powerful mind, positioned toward creating success.

As you continue to explore and discover the true potential of the mental factors, consider how the mental aspects of success can support each of the three elements of leadership success.

- **Self-Leadership** — "Includes your ability to understand the power of thoughts created by your beliefs and perceptions, which generate thought forms and powerful emotions. You learn to choose thoughts that are success-building instead of success-blocking.

- **Self-Management** — "Establishes a practice to increase your skill set for managing success-oriented core thoughts and offers support and momentum to your primary desires. You understand that how you use your mental faculties to engage, create, clear, clarify, decide, focus and intuitively live in the present determines your level of success.

- **Self-Mastery** — Demonstrates a self-mastery mindset and includes focusing in on the leadership presence and the ability to be fully present in the moment. You have full access to personal power, potential and resources needed to create and experience success.

Maximizing Your Mental Factor to Increase Success—
Your brain's ability to function optimally in relation to a task, activity or situation enhances clarity and engagement. The clearer you are about what you need to do to accomplish a specific activity or to achieve success in your role. The more you eliminate indecision and uncertainty, the more present you will be and the more you will engage your mental faculties.

What insights came up for you in the mental factor section? Can you recall an experience when you were fully engaged, present, and in the flow of energy toward an activity, effort or experience? Identify the key ingredients of that experience and record them in your journal. What was different from other experiences? What actions contributed to that experience? What were the contributing factors to experiencing those moments of success?

Before moving to the next energetic success factor, identify at least one area of your mental routines you'd like to enhance:

_____

_____

Now, select a new ritual that will support your ability to exceed your previous experiences:

_____

_____

THE PHYSICAL SUCCESS FACTOR

Essentially the physical factor is your ability to perform an activity or task to ensure your success. Out of the combined six factors, the physical factor is most often focused upon as a vital path to success. Most individuals will look to physical aspects before considering any of the other factors. It is understandable why there is so much emphasis placed on physical well-being because when you feel vibrant and active, you have the best opportunity to experience increased levels of success. The physical factor is the foundation that bridges its purpose and power with each of the other factors to create a renewed potential for increased success. When your physical body cannot function optimally it depletes your vibrancy and energy. It is much easier to notice the condition of your energy from a physical perspective compared to each of the other five factors.

It's easy to see when an individual is lacking energy or if they are tired and limited in their capacity to excel. You may notice it in their voice as they sometimes lack the energy and volume to communicate effectively with others. You might see it in their posture or the way they walk and carry themselves throughout their work day. You may experience a person's expression that conveys messages of sadness, fear, worry, and distress instead of their usual presence of excitement, passion and enthusiasm. These expressions represent physical energy.

When you focus on the impact of the physical energetic factor, there are many elements to consider; including your overall health and well-being, your weight, endurance, sleep patterns, exercise rituals, breathing patterns, nutritional habits, vital indicators and self-image, to name a few. This is a general overview of the physical factors to promote awareness of the contributing factors to success. Each of the areas included in the physical faculties should be broken down and reviewed for a customized plan to optimize and maximize each of their potential benefits.

Inspired Discovery Exercise

Create a routine of scanning your physical energy. Notice if your body is holding any tension or stress and take notice of your posture. Notice how you walk, sit, speak, communicate with others. Take note of your overall presence and how you are using your physical presence to build success or block success.

Think back to a time in your career when you had to give a presentation or talk in front of a group of other individuals, and you felt tense or may not have gotten enough sleep the night before. How did that impact your ability to experience success?

Now consider a time when you were physically vibrant and at the top of your game. What steps did you take to ensure this physical vibrancy? Did you eat healthy, exercise, sleep soundly? Was your presence energized by passion and a relaxed, pleasing and inspiring tone? What made this experience different? As you consider success and explore the many impacts that might alter your success, it is most helpful to break down each of the six energetic success factors that contribute to your success states.

Notice how the physical factors contribute to each of the three elements of leadership success.

- **Self-Leadership** — includes the personal awareness, responsibility and willingness to take ownership of your physical presence and consider the impact it has on your ability to perform and create success.

- **Self-Management** — includes the commitment, dedication and desire to carry out a plan of practices, rituals and routines to ensure the physical factors are all available as needed to perform the task at hand.

- **Self-Mastery** — includes the ability to master the physical factors into a state of maximized success. It ensures that all physical resources are functioning in an optimal condition and available to you. This is where your presence is most empowered with a concentration of the physical energy on doing and the spiritual energy on being. Both aspects of your presence are combined to enhance performance.

Maximizing Your Physical Factor to Increase Success —
Your ability to stay in tune with what your body needs to excel is essential. Your physical power to accomplish any activity is necessary to experience success. There are many resources now available to support you in creating physical vibrancy. Some of these include electronic awareness devices with reminders to ensure that you move physically, to inspire increased activity as well as readings that depict the quality of your health status.

As you review the awareness presented on this topic of the physical success factor, take a personal assessment and consider how your physical health is impacting your ability to experience success or limit success.

THE SPIRITUAL SUCCESS FACTOR

This presents the energy of meaning and purpose, the *why* behind your sense of fulfillment or contribution and the sustaining power that drives you toward a state of self-mastery. The spiritual factor includes your sense of purpose and overall meaning in all aspects of your life, integrating intangible and immeasurable qualities that influence your behavior and energy. Leaders often overlook the spiritual factors necessary for creating success. Essentially, it is how well you, as a leader, align your vision with your sense of purpose, which is the key ingredient to mastering your success.

As you expand upon the many aspects of the spiritual factor, you will assess your ability to connect with purpose and your alignment of values, visions and goals. You will determine if you can reach the fulfillment of your desires and pinpoint your sources of inspiration and the motivators required to fuel your success. These are key aspects of the spiritual factor, vital elements that determine the potential to excel and experience long-term sustainable success.

The spiritual factor is a primary reason why individuals don't reach their desired goals. From my own personal experience and the work that I do with clients, individuals who are routinely struggling to reach their goals without success find there is a spiritual factor that is missing or misaligned, preventing them from excelling.

Have you ever heard the phrase, "Who is whispering inspiration in your ear?" This query describes the energy of the spiritual factor; it's what drives you to exceed your expectations. It is the fuel and electrifying energy that ignites you to be bold, take chances, and uncover new experiences to excel. It is the why behind the inspired action and the motivation to keep moving toward your goals.

I believe the spiritual factor is missing in traditional roles of leadership success and is a primary opportunity for growth and a core element of authentic success. This is the energy that conveys confidence, connection, trust, balance, fulfillment, determination, commitment, resilience and a greater vision.

As you reflect upon the spiritual factor and look to identify it in your work life, ask yourself the following questions.

- Do you have a defined purpose prevalent in the work you're doing?

- How are your values being expressed in your work? What core values are missing?

- How does your work showcase your authenticity and natural talents?

- Does your work give you the fulfillment of your burning desire to succeed? If so, in what ways?

- How well do you balance your work and life responsibilities?

Consider how the spiritual factor shows up in each of the three leadership success elements:

- **Self-Leadership** — This is the state of spiritual awareness and the self-realization of the role spirituality plays in success. Success includes internal and external success, and the role of self-leadership is the bridge that connects these two aspects in an authentic and empowering way.

- **Self-Management** — Your ability to manage your spiritual resources to ensure that you maintain purpose in your roles and balance in your lives at work and beyond. To establish trust in yourselves and the companies you work for and the people with whom you interact. It is your sense of unity and connection, creativity and inspiration. It is your ability to create a strong spiritual foundation in which to drive all other aspects of your desires toward your success.

- **Self-Mastery** — A state of sacredness, authenticity and presence filled with respect, honor, awareness, wisdom, and inner peace. It is found in your ability to stand up, speak your truth, express your authenticity and step into the unknown. Think of a spiritual warrior in the workplace who has shown a wisdom far beyond the norm, a spirit that is unwavering, and a passion filled with potential and a most profound connection to self and others.

When you explore the spiritual factors, you may have the tendency to think of religion as the point of reference. However, your purpose in this context is to increase awareness around the overall spiritual qualities within the experience of success. To pinpoint the anabolic qualities of inner peace, contribution, purpose, passion, connection, inspiration and similar experiences.

Maximizing Your Spiritual Factor to Increase Success—
Your spiritual factors are a direct correlation to what you specifically want to do and how you want to do it. They are the drivers, motivators and inspirations that identify answers to the question, "Why do I desire success?" **Spiritual factors are signposts that lead you toward fulfillment and away from frustration.** As you continue to look for examples of how your spiritual factors influence your daily routines, bring your attention to experiences when you feel a conflict or disconnect with what you're doing. Notice situations in which you feel a lack of purpose and waning passion. Pay attention to the times in which you feel direct conflict with any one of your primary values. At this point, I would invite you to begin a new journey of discovery to uncover how the spiritual factors are impacting your work day and how they can improve the optimized and maximized success you so deeply desire.

The spiritual factor is the doorway to uncovering the experiences that contribute to the pain, frustration, and lack of fulfillment in your work life. Your spiritual factors provide missing ingredients in your recipe for success. It helps you understand why some people struggle and others excel. This spiritual alignment is the pathway to authentic leadership. It is the key to self-awareness and gaining clarity on what wants to happen. Your spiritual factors are each an indicator of what you want to experience more of and what experiences you want less of in your work life.

THE SOCIAL SUCCESS FACTOR

Up to this point you have been introduced to each of the internal energetic success factors. Now you are ready to redirect your attention to the external energetic factors, the social and environmental energetic success factors.

The social factor includes your ability to connect, communicate and create with other people. It includes your attitude toward others, how you influence them or are influenced by them, your ability to lead and to follow as well as your desired level of social interaction and how it impacts your energetic state. Are you energized by others and do you gain energy from them as extroverts, or do you feel depleted when you spend too much time in the presence of others as introverts often do?

The social factor enhances your state of success and engagement. Once you understand how to maximize your social energy, you will realize the perfect balance between spending time with others and spending moments alone in rejuvenation. Imagine an automobile's gas tank as an example of your social energetic state. Social energy has the potential to fill your gas tank to full when you engage in an energetic exchange with others. It also has the potential to deplete your fuel tank, leaving you "on empty" when you don't honor your own authentic tendencies. It's important to know where you stand on the social scale of the gas tank gauge and honor that awareness.

The social factor includes how you manage your energy in relation to others, knowing when to listen and when to share. It is the way you communicate and interact with others, determining if you will support or compete with others. It is your ability to nurture and be present to honor the other person(s) and surround yourself by like-minded people. Ideally, when you optimize your social energy strengths, you understand your core energetic needs, and you recognize the social needs required to sustain your social energy. When you lead from this renewed state of awareness, you have a vast ability to support, inspire, influence, and connect with others in ways that are extremely empowering.

On a scale of one to ten, with one indicating no success and ten being a total success, how would you rate your success level in the social factors? Do you have empowering, supportive coworkers with whom you enjoy working? Do you enjoy a network of like-minded professionals who inspire you to excel? Are mentors available to keep you stimulated and engaged? How are the social factors playing out in your work day? Where are the areas of improvements? What part of the social factors influence you the most? How can you shift this experience to have more success-building opportunities?

As an Executive Leadership Success Coach and career leadership professional, I would not be serving you if I did not call out the social factor of listening as a primary element of success. Your ability to listen subjectively by sensing the feeling, objectively with logic and intuitively with deepened awareness enables you to discover the energy that lives beneath the words being spoken. Listening provides a keen insight into the information that is driving the discussion, the needs that are yearning for acknowledgment, the solutions to problems that have been ongoing and the values that drive your need to excel.

Leaders who have mastered the skills to be present with others, listening to the energy and tone of voice, observing the body language, and noting the messages that reside just beneath the words being spoken create an enormous impact on success. If you're serious about mastering your leadership presence and want to move the mark of your experienced success, consider studying these topics more fully. Hire a leadership success coach to guide you or a mentor who has mastered the energy of conversation. This is an area that offers one of the greatest aspects to creating success.

You have reviewed several core elements of the social factor and the importance they have in creating success. Consider how social factors impact each of the three elements to leadership success.

- **Self-Leadership** — opens the door for self-awareness and your willingness to recognize other individuals outside yourselves when making strategic choices and decisions. At this level, your social skills increase, and you become more adept at considering the needs of others and the impact you have on them.

- **Self-Management** — includes your ability to manage your energy when you are in connection with others, understanding and honoring your own needs to spend more time or less time with others, and knowing the impact that your connection has on your energetic resources. It includes the emotional intelligence and awareness of how to balance your actions that impact others. A realization of knowing when to lead and follow, when to speak or listen.

- **Self-Mastery** — focuses on your presence, who you are being in relation to others. Your ability to be present and focused upon the other person's needs within an encounter or current conversation. As self-masters, you learn to release the need to interrupt a conversation or to get your needs met; you are fully present with the individual engaged with you, listening deeply on all levels to ensure the other person feels acknowledged, heard, understood and received. You are comfortable with silence within an exchange of conversation. You show the ability to be present fully in each moment, communicating your own ideas and desires while offering support to others.

When you have the skills and awareness to determine which social situations work best for you and are confident in your ability to navigate different social interactions, you have the power to proactively create situations of success.

Inspired Discovery Exercise

Reflect upon a time when you attended a meeting or social situation where you noticed feeling uncomfortable communicating with others. Maybe you experienced a level of tension and anxiety in your ability to express your thoughts with others or felt rushed trying to communicate your ideas before others share their perspectives. As you reflect on this experience, notice what happened and try to identify the key influencing factors that contributed to your discomfort? How might you change the way you responded?

Also, recall an experience when you felt fully engaged and present with other individuals as they communicated their ideas to you. What contributed to your sense of ease? What about the situation was different? How can you include this awareness to excel in future experiences?

Maximizing Your Social Factor to Increase Success—
Your ability to identify the right balance of social interaction and connection with others is vital to your success. Knowing which situations inspire you and which ones disempower you is the key. Your ability to offer support to others while also finding sources of personal support is important to maintain the inner and outer balance needed. Develop a skill for sensing energy of situations and others. Learn to detect the catabolic success-blocking energy and the anabolic success-building energy as a model for identifying like-minded teams and professionals with whom you will thrive.

THE ENVIRONMENTAL SUCCESS FACTOR

The sixth energetic success factor is the environmental factor, which includes the settings and conditions in which you work and perform. It identifies the tangible physical elements that impact your energy and success. Your environment has a large impact on your ability to create success; it determines if you feel comfortable, energetic and at ease or if you feel stressed, tense or lacking vitality. As you consider the list of potential factors included in the environmental conditions, it is important to note that some of them are in our control while others may not be. Assessing each situation for the environmental factors in relation to your ability to create maximized success is essential.

Some factors that impact your success are the overall conditions of your workspace, the surroundings near your work area, the temperature in the building, lighting and noise levels, as well as the availability of technology resources and equipment — Also factor in access to general amenities such as food, water and restrooms. Each person's environmental factors are different; however, it is important that you create a workspace that allows you to focus and feel connected, creative, inspired, innovative, and any other aspect that is needed to maximize your success potential.

To review, sensing the energy of your space can offer insight into what's promoting success and what areas require additional support. Your ability to be resilient and identify the proper environments in which to thrive is key. Knowing your preferred daily rituals and rhythms are also helpful. Uncover the best time of the day to be productive and identify when you are most energized and inspired. Assess periods of the day when you slow down and need rest. Your ability to realize the many impacts that your work environment has on your work life is important to maximizing success.

Considering the impacts of environmental factors, explore how they impact each of the three elements to leadership success.

- **Self-Leadership** — A strong self-leader shows the ability to act and use increased self-responsibility for creating the optimal work space and conditions that have the proper resources to experience success.

- **Self-Management** — Managing all the many factors required to optimize and maximize the success potential is the main objective. The ability to adjust resources (adding some, removing others) creates the proper harmony and alignment for an ideal setting.

- **Self-Mastery** — Creating a strong connection between the leader and the surrounding environment reflects a vision of alignment and success. These environments become alive, inspiring the leader who lives within them to be success-oriented, and they function as a source of inspiration for others who experience the settings.

Inspired Discovery Exercise

Take a personal assessment of each of the factors listed above, review each of your surrounding areas and physical resources required to support your experience of success. When you enter your workspace do you feel inspired, creative and content to spend time there? Or does your space lack vitality and inspiration? Select a favorite notebook or journal to keep with you throughout your work day and note environmental factors that add to your comfort and an overall feeling of success. Record those areas that need improvement or adjustment to maximize their success potential. Use your sensory skills and your intuitive powers to sense the energy of each part of your surroundings. Notice ideas and messages that come up as you monitor your connection and fulfillment associated with each of your environmental factors.

Maximizing Your Environmental Factor to Increase Success—
As you monitor and assess each element of your environmental factors, don't forget to monitor the beliefs you have about the space you live in. Establishing empowering beliefs about your space and your ability to succeed is important. If you have a belief that is impeding your success, consider viewing it from many different perspectives.
Ask yourself:

- Is this belief true?

- Is it true for myself only or would others believe it to be true as well?

- Is it possible that others may perceive the environmental factors from a different perspective?

Identify beliefs and intentions that add energy, strength, and creative power to your spaces and notice the renewed ease, connection and inspiration that surfaces.

Section V presents the pathways to experiencing the energy of limitless success through becoming the Inspired Authentic Leader.

Section Five...

Experiencing the Energy of Success

Increase Your Success Potential

17. Becoming Empowered Through Self-Mastery

When you live and lead from a place of increased awareness and a leadership presence that evokes a state of self-mastery, you are empowered with the energy of success.

This energy is aligned and activated to help you achieve your desires and goals. This is a presence that is authentic, filled with a sense of ease and free from worry or lack of confidence. It is a presence filled with a deeper sense of knowing— an energy that is prevailing and filled with a potential to embrace each moment as a new opportunity to experience success.

You are ready to build a long-term practice and a renewed being state that automatically resonates at higher levels of success, making you less likely to experience a decrease in energy. Begin implementing this awareness through practice and expand upon any insights that emerge. Each time you tune in to the energy of the moment, your awareness will evolve. In time, the practice itself will become a natural part of your daily rituals.

Your Self-Mastery Practice for Experiencing Success

To become masterful at experiencing a vibrant success-oriented state of being, consider the 5R's of Success: Reconnect, Reclaim, Rediscover, Reignite and Renew. The following chart depicts a support tool that helps generate and maintain higher levels of energy. This process functions as a *"self-mastery practice"* that can be used as a guide for aligning your energy and state of being with heightened conscious awareness.

The 5 R's of Workplace Success

Reconnect	To become aware and accepting of what is
Reclaim	To make conscious choices and trust the process
Re-discover	To re-discover your true nature, being authentic, fearless with confidence
Re-ignite	To re-ignite your passion with a deeper sense of connection
Renew	To be in the moment and 100% engaged

To apply the 5 R's of Success process fully, explore the true potential of each aspect:

Reconnect

To sustain high levels of success-oriented energy you must become masterful at hitting the pause button to slow down and turn inward. This is an invitation to become the *observer* of your own life and let go of judgment of yourself and others. Reconnect is the practice of being aware of the leadership success states and understanding how they are impacting you as an individual and the people who work with you. This practice combines awareness with acceptance and releasing judgment to promote inner peace, harmony, ease and flow. You create experiences and associations with higher states of success-oriented energy.

Reconnecting to yourself and living from a peaceful, centered state is the first step toward maximizing your experience of success. Start your work day with the practice of reconnecting to your self-mastery state. This practice of mastery and impact teaches you to realize who you are at your core being and to reconnect to your greatest desire and potential. It is an opportunity to partner with higher levels of energy to keep you aligned and enlivened with creativity and fueled with the potential of powerful and productive energy.

One way to incorporate the practice of reconnection, self-awareness and acceptance is to begin your day with 15 to 20 minutes of meditation that promotes self-reflection. This one simple practice can be a game changer to success, as it quiets the mind and clears the mental clutter. Self-reflection provides a sense of expanded awareness and a feeling of being grounded in our true nature of pure potential. There are many forms of meditation. Most include sitting quietly and focusing on the breath as it flows slowly and steadily with each inhalation and exhalation. You may choose a meditation practice that includes a mantra or statement of inspiration that is designed to release the mental clutter and create a rhythm of awareness.

If meditation is not ideal for you, create a practice of reading a daily inspiring passage, followed by journaling about the messages that resonate most deeply. If you dedicate a few moments in the morning to reconnect to your state of being and inner awareness, it will provide support throughout your work day with measurable results. Think of a large tree that has massive roots deeply entrenched in vibrant soil that surrounds it and provides structure and support. This support offers the tree strength, power, and long-term vitality just as self-reflection and meditation offer those benefits to you.

Reclaim

This is your capacity to reclaim your own inner power and practice self-responsibility to make conscious decisions for your success or take ownership for the lack of success you experience. If you fail to maintain control over your own destiny, then you become the victim of your circumstances. Instead, you must become masterful at directing your energy toward your goals and visions. A key factor to experiencing success is your ability to become the driver of your own success and choose each moment on how to respond to each situation.

In previous chapters, you were introduced to the importance of choosing your responses instead of reacting to triggered events or allowing situations to choose for you. Reclaiming your power roots itself in self-leadership and increases your ability to make consciously informed decisions. You return to a way of being that allows you to release the outcome and to openly trust the process to unfold naturally, effortlessly and with ease. This experience is an expression of a true state of self-mastery.

One way to incorporate the practice of reclaiming into your daily rituals is to play a game with yourself and monitor your ability to decide without hesitation. Record how many times you respond to a situation instead of reacting. Keep a journal on situations that trigger you and spend a few moments identifying the root cause of your reaction. What was the trigger? What might have contributed to this reaction?

Another way is to play a game called *Respond vs. React*. When non-life-threatening situations occur, notice how long it takes for you to respond to the situation. Does your first response include a planned response, or do you routinely react? As you go about your work day, notice if you are most often in the driver's seat, choosing your response or in a passenger's seat, reacting to the situation. Where does your power live?

This playful exercise is informative if you open fully to its potential. Become masterful at making conscious decisions naturally and minimize the urge to react in each moment. Visualize your reactions as a pressure cooker that is releasing so much steam and pressure it forces the lid to release the pressure that was once being contained. When you react, you lose your power. When you respond, you maintain and energize your power and potential.

Re-discover

Your ability to live and lead from a self-mastery state of being includes staying open to the magic in the moment of discovery. As you view each situation with openness and eyes of wonder, ask yourself, "What wants to happen here?" Ask yourself "What if?" and "Why not?" When you live and lead from a place of rediscovering your true nature as pure success potential, you become fearless, confident in your own skin, filled with authenticity, inspiration and impact. When you lead from a place of authenticity, you experience a sense of ease and effortless power. As you experience each moment through the eyes of discovery, you move from a "doing" state that often requires force, into a "being" state of flow and ease.

To incorporate the rediscovery practice into your daily life, create a practice of identifying new experiences to challenge yourself and promote new awareness. Create a new neural network connection that keeps your mental capacity strong. This daily challenge might include taking a new road on your way to work, selecting a new flavor of coffee at the local coffee shop, trying out a new software tool to learn its capability, or extending a lunch invitation to a coworker you haven't had time to get to know. The ideas are endless, the practice is simple. Find new ways to rediscover your true nature of being authentic, confident, bold and fearless. The goal is to get outside your comfort zone to experience, explore and expand your awareness.

Re-ignite }

The practice of reigniting includes your ability to feel a sense of connection to yourselves, to others you interact with along with the environment and world that surrounds you. You transform your perspective from an individual experience to a unified and global perspective. As you take ownership of your destiny, you become passionate, driven and inspired to create your ideal vision of success. You experience a deeper connection, and as empowered leaders, you feel the support, harmony and unity of all the other resources.

When you use your energy to come into a natural state of flow, no separation exists between the doing state and the being state. At the core of this combined synergy, you experience the natural skills to take inspired action and embrace behaviors that are fueled by higher forms of energy. These experiences often include feelings described as purposeful, passionate, presence, flow, ease and effortless— to name a few examples.

Like a wheel that contains many individual spokes joined together to support the entire wheel, the energy of reigniting your connection to all things is a true practice of self-mastery. When you align your focus of connection with a vision of harmony, unity and synergy, you experience a holistic or "whole" perspective. Within this alignment, synchronicity and happy coincidences occur and increase your potential to experience maximized success.

One idea to consider in applying the practice of reigniting is to make a conscious decision to experience new connections each day. Capture a few ideas on how this might work for you. Create a practice of self-connection, as discussed in the reconnect phase detailed previously. Your ability to connect with others and the surrounding environment is essential. Identify a plan to dedicate a small part of your day to connecting with others. What might this look and feel like? Consider scheduling one or two days out of your week to have lunch with coworkers, clients and other professionals. During this time try to stay present without distraction and experience the other person fully, listening actively to the many aspects of their shared experiences.

Another way to incorporate the potential of reigniting your connection with others is to establish a ritual for arriving home at the end of the work day. How can you use your first few moments to ensure that you make a deeper connection to your spouse and family members? Take into consideration the environment that surrounds you and the impact it has on your ability to feel connected.

One way to start your day feeling connected is a walk or jog in nature, spending a few moments outside noticing the trees, flowers and animals. Scheduling time to experience the outdoor environment can help you feel rooted, aligned with your core energy and outside the mental chatter that keeps you stuck in a success-blocking state. Your success depends on your ability to connect with yourself more fully, to experience a connection with others on deeper levels and to connect to the world that surrounds, supports and sustains you.

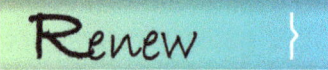

The last of the 5 R's of self-mastery practices opens the door to the state of being truly masterful. You will increase your awareness and experiences to be fully present in the moment and engaged on an energetic level, free from distractions. Being fully present allows the mind to connect with the body automatically to take action, free from stressful deliberation.

As Inspired Authentic Leaders, you will know that true power and potential lives only within each moment, each opportunity to experience 100 percent potential for maximized success.

Renewing your connection to your fully present state and aligning your energy with the opportunity in the moment requires awareness, commitment and practice. Releasing your attachment to projected outcomes opens the door and invites in the potential of *"what wants to happen."* Your ability to release judgment and replace it with observation and a willingness to partner with true potential is key to success.

All life experiences are necessary and vital to success, just like a recipe that includes many core ingredients to create the desired dish. As you fully engage with the moment of each experience, your willingness to buy in and become motivated increases your energy and supports your actions. You become fully committed, free of doubt, inspired and renewed with a courageous sense of confidence. **To include this renewal phase into your daily practice, consider the following example of the athlete in training.**

Imagine an athlete training to run a high intensity short distance race that requires maximum energy to kick-start momentum and sustain the runner all the way to the finish line. How might the inability to focus on the present moment impact the athlete's success?

What if the athlete succumbs to feelings of self-doubt or beliefs focused on failure? How might these thoughts and feelings impact the athlete's success? **Your ability to lead yourself in each moment, fully present, aware and in control of your thoughts, feelings and energetic qualities will pave your path to optimal success.**

As you use the awareness of the athlete preparing for a peak performance, spend a few moments identifying your own core essential elements for success. List five to ten examples of how you might prepare yourself for a potential performance of success.

1. _____

2. _____

3. _____

4. _____

5. _____

Calling Out Your Superpowers to Activate the Energy of Success

What if you had the ability to activate your energy and anchor your presence in a success-oriented masterful state regardless of the circumstance that presented itself? I compare this experience to a superhero putting on their super power armor to energize their potential for sustaining success. Every emotion, situation, and energetic state you desire can be self-generated. You never have to wait for something to happen for you to experience this desire... simply be it, act it out, turn it on, create it and embrace it fully.

What if you had an automated process available to activate your core state of success energy that aligns your focus, energetic capacity and awareness to heightened levels of effectiveness? This heightened state of awareness and presence is the opposite of a fight-or-flight state you might experience during survival circumstances. Instead, this experience is a place of power, authenticity, knowingness, strength, and focus that is rooted firmly in the energy of success. During this experience you transform yourself to live, lead, and unleash your greatest potential. Just like an energetic switch of awareness that gets activated in the moment, we show the ability to move from the place in which we acknowledge a new desire to a place of empowerment that is rooted in tremendous potential. How does this concept resonate with you?

To begin this exercise, reflect upon a few of the core qualities and traits you might need to experience for an optimized and maximized presence of success. Explore potential ideas for creating a practice of being present in the moment. Begin to consider a ritual you can use in the moment to promote a centered, empowered alignment. Your breath is one of the most powerful resources to bring your attention into a focused, present state.

Practice creating your own personalized success state, which is a state of being you can turn on and step into any time you choose. To do this, you may start the creative exercise by focusing on a superhero such as Wonder Woman, Batman, or the energy of a warrior or super hero to get your creative juices flowing. These heroes often put on their suit of armor to embody a superhero power. What if you developed a similar practice that supported you in aligning and embodying the energy of success? A presence that is attuned with and fueled by feelings of a superpower and energetic qualities that reflect success. Have fun with this exercise. The more you experience your own empowered state, the less time it will take to activate this personal presence during challenging or high potential encounters.

To help define your empowered success state, consider:

- o What does the superhero image of yourself look like?
- o What qualities are shown?
- o What type of actions does the superhero take?
- o What is different about the superhero's actions?
- o How is their energy being represented in their presence?

Notice tone of voice and overall energy of their presence. Create a visual representation that includes the key elements to your own personal superhero example of success. Once you have a good description and feel a resonant connection with it, identify a way to energize it and invite it to become more alive and exude a potent level of energy. Consider giving it a nickname or name that denotes a core quality of yourself that evokes power and strength.

Your superhero represents a strong version of your most powerful, purposeful self. Next, identify a process that activates its energy. For example, a word like "command," a specific stance or a movement that activates your awareness of its presence. As you continue to experiment with this concept, you will discover a deeper connection and a reduction in the time it takes to transform your energy into this success-oriented state. This transformational energy shift is an exercise that creates awareness on how to transform each situation into a success-producing opportunity. As time unfolds, you will no longer have to remind yourself to focus on the activation process. Instead, you will transition from an ordinary state of energy into an escalated powerful state of success-producing energy that happens automatically and is driven by a sense of ease.

Personally, one of my methods of activating a centered, balanced, and powerful state of energy is to practice the Warrior II (Virabhadrasana II) yoga pose.

In this pose, the feet are balanced with the front foot pointed forward and the knee slightly bent, aligned over the toes. The other leg extends back, straight and elongated to create a sturdy, balanced stance. The arms are both open and extended outward over the feet to take on the presence of an empowered warrior. The drishti (focal point of the gaze) is the front fingers. The energy activated in this moment is powerful, strong, calming and enlivening.

Another example that can be used is a command that initiates the presence of energy and centers your awareness in the moment. Imagine a small square or circle in front of you that is fully activated and empowered with vibrant energy and the expression of your superhero power. In this state, the feet are both firmly planted on the floor; the body aligned, shoulders relaxed, breath softened, and the eyes focused toward the goal. This is a place of ease, with a feeling of being centered and confident. You know that regardless of what situation surfaces, you have the awareness and presence of energy to create the success you desire. Within this square, a presence of power exists, and you become unstoppable and deeply successful. This is the energy of success.

Your mode of activation does not need to be extreme; it may include a mudra, which is a small hand gesture to remind yourself of the shift in energy.

Each of the self-mastery practices are helpful to maintain a high level of success-producing energy. They are each powerful in their potential, and collectively they bring you into a self-mastery state that is aligned and engaged with success. They are designed to energize and increase your purpose and passion for increased potential.

When you reconnect with your true potential, becoming aware and in acceptance of who you are as a leader, you reclaim your power to make conscious choices and lead from a place of trusting the process. As you lead from a place of surrender and trust that releases the defined outcome, you rediscover your increased potential to feel more authentic, fearless, and confident in your journey, which reignites your passion and gives you a deeper sense of connection with yourself and others that surround you. As you continue your experience with living and leading with the state of self-mastery, you experience a renewed energy that supports you in living in the present moment, fully engaged with each activity, situation, or circumstance that comes your way. You know no matter what happens throughout the course of your work day, you have the tools, temperament, and tenacity to transform each moment into a success-oriented, success-producing experience.

Using the practices of self-mastery detailed above will activate a discovery process to uncover what's supporting you with creating success and what actions or activities are preventing you from experiencing success. Consider playing the role of a workplace detector that looks through the lens of awareness for workplace success. Take notice of how you use your energy each day to respond to activities and circumstances. Create a practice of recording behaviors, reactions, triggers, responses, expressions and other patterns of experiences and notice how they impact your day.

As you take notice of your energy and how it is used to transform and interact within your work life and the impact it has on your daily success, you will see the patterns, behaviors and tendencies that are most prevalent. When you increase your awareness and incorporate the tools and concepts provided throughout this book, you will have the power and potential to create, sustain and maximize your momentum toward creating and experiencing your ideal vision of success.

Bringing it All Together

To review, this section on self-mastery leadership focuses on maximizing your energy to ensure that you maintain the highest states of increased success. It offers the experience of self-mastery as a partnership for maximizing the energy available in the moment and your ability to utilize your energy and resources for increased performance, engagement and overall effectiveness.

This chapter identifies the game changers of success and uncovers the six energetic success factors that have the potential to either contribute to or limit your experience of success. The 5 R's of Success provide a self-mastery practice and a method for maintaining higher levels of success-oriented energy.

You have been invited to explore the path to optimizing any level of success. This exploration becomes the enhancer that establishes a distinction between routine experiences of success and those experiences when we are masterful in our ability to create success.

As you begin to consider each of the factors revealed within this chapter, you may resonate with some and not others. Listen closely to the ones that resonate most deeply, while also staying open to using others as you continue to expand your awareness. You are the Inspired Authentic Leader who has taken the journey to creating more maximized success in your work life and the life in which you live and lead others.

Key Takeaways:
Using the Concepts Discovered in the Self-Mastery Section

o The four levels of engagement, the "DSCO" model, was discussed at the beginning of the self-mastery section. It identifies levels of engagement and where your energy exists.

o The coin theory explored in this module anchors your energy and awareness in either the problem or the solution.

o Embrace the game changers to success by uncovering the potential for each of the six Energetic Success Factors that either create success or decrease your potential for success.

o Maintain higher levels of performance and engagement using the 5 R's of Success as a support tool for generating and maintaining higher levels of energy.

o Activate the energy of success and create a super power figure to turn on your energetic power and potential to experience success.

You have made a lot of progress through your journey from self-leadership to self-mastery and your ability to be exceptional and to become the Inspired Authentic Leader.

You now realize that you have everything necessary to experience your vision of desired success. You have the presence, tools and capacity needed to experience an empowered state of energy and to fuel the overall impact you desire to become an exceptional leader.

The next chapter takes a deeper dive into being exceptional and becoming the Inspired Authentic Leader, a state of self-mastery that is highly skilled, aware, enlightened and ready to embrace the potential for maximized success.

18. Being Exceptional as the Inspired Authentic Leader – Experiencing a Zest for Success

You have taken the journey to becoming the Inspired Authentic Leader, a state of self-mastery that is highly skilled, aware, enlightened and ready to embrace the potential for renewed experiences of success.

By reading this book and completing the exercises offered, you effectively explored self-awareness, which opened the door to self-leadership and the seven states of leadership success. You discovered how to manage your energy and attitude by identifying the desired leadership success state you wish to experience during each moment of the day. You understand the impact and potential outcome that each state offers and the required skills to utilize each state as needed to generate the success you desire. In the self-mastery sections, you delved deeply into the seven energetic success factors that hold the potential to either enhance your success or limit your success.

The awareness discovered in the sections about self-management provide keen insight into identifying your state of being by carefully considering, "Who you are being?" in each moment and how that state of being impacts your success. You have gained awareness for pinpointing the experiences that build success and those that block success.

Each aspect discovered in the three areas of self-leadership, self-management and self-mastery is monumental to achieving success. Underneath the core of these three areas lies the underpinning of our time together, your ability to live and lead with a leadership presence and state of being that reflects success. There is a new realization that everything you experience, every situation, circumstance and event you experience, is a projection of your conditioned self. This realization means you now have a choice whether to manage each situation or allow the situation to manage you.

With this renewed understanding, you are empowered to choose higher states of leadership success and freed from the illusions and limitations that reside in the lower states of leadership. You have become the Inspired Authentic Leader who demonstrates an expression of freedom with a sense of deeper fulfillment and increased flow. You have been given the awareness and necessary tools required to release yourself from the energy busters of limiting beliefs and the increased ability to live from a place of being exceptional. This is the home of your greatest desires and the expression of your ideal vision of success.

During our time together, you have explored each of the seven states of leadership success and the associated impact and outcome that each state offers. This awareness empowers individuals to utilize the energy of each state as needed to create their desired outcome. You have the opportunity to engage fully with others in communication that resonates with each person's state of being and the ability to explore and experience life through the different lens that each state provides.

Our journey together provided the opportunity to experience each leadership success state and discover the navigation tools required to uncover your true potential as the Inspired Authentic Leader. This state of self-mastery utilizes the presence and expression related to the higher states of leadership success most often experienced in the opportunist, creator and mastery success states. The Inspired Authentic Leader is the title I gave to this experience of self-mastery. It functions as the face of being exceptional — being the greatest version of yourself as a strong self-leader and self-master for creating your own desired success. The title is not as important as the experience. The experience is everything; it is life-changing. When you experience a state of being that is open to each moment, free of judgment and filled with the confidence and knowingness that you have everything needed to create your desired experiences, you elevate yourself to increased potential that reflects the qualities of success you've always yearned to experience. Your acceptance of the idea that you embody the fullest potential to experience success in every moment frees you from waiting and wondering when success will unfold in your life.

Experiencing a Zest for Success

Your ability to determine what you desire and to align that vision with the state of being and character qualities related to your thoughts, feelings, actions and associated results is key to your success. Each leadership success state provides a choice and a state of being that contains a related experience of success. Using the energy that exists within each moment allows you to choose who you will be and how you will respond to each new opportunity.

Now is the time to apply these principles to each of your daily roles and responsibilities. Just like a seed that will not grow without the proper water and nutrition, your commitment to using this knowledge to enhance the way you show up for your work life will determine your level of success.

The ability to excel beyond traditional forms of success includes the willingness to go outside your comfort zone. That means letting go of the structured pre-planned vision you've been holding onto for so long and partner with bold curiosity to determine "what wants to happen." The opportunity for true long-term sustainable success lives in the shadows of the unknown and offers us the opportunity to create success in each moment while releasing the attachment to a pre-defined outcome.

Regardless of the goal you are trying to achieve, when you hold fast to a desire that contains a pre-defined outcome, you limit the energy and opportunity to experience another outcome that equals or exceeds your expectations.

As you embrace and implement the strategies of self-leadership, self-management and self-mastery, your leadership presence as the Inspired Authentic Leader comes to life. You understand the impact that each decision has on your ability to feel engaged, empowered and aligned with renewed potential. You now know how to use your energy to create optimized and maximized success.

Activating the Energy of Success

*The way to become a powerful leader
is to understand the power of energy.*

Your energy is the one thing that makes the most impact. The way you utilize the energy of presence, attitude, choice and decision will contribute to your experience of success. As the Inspired Authentic Leader, you are a leader that is fueled by the energy of success. You have a deep inner knowing that success and the higher states of leadership already reside within you and are available to help you excel beyond routine concepts of success.

Once you begin to observe the energy of each moment, sensing the ease and flow or the limitations and feelings of resistance, you realize that you are either aligned with the energy of success or outside of its flow. The gift of being the Inspired Authentic Leader resides in the opportunity to live and lead from the higher states of expanded awareness. Struggle is an illusion that limits your awareness and performance and prevents you from experiencing your ideal vision of success. As an Inspired Authentic Leader, you have a natural capacity to tap into the higher qualities that emanate success and use these experiences to create and sustain the goal of experiencing limitless success.

When you embrace a state of self-mastery and become the Inspired Authentic Leader, you commit to a leadership presence, a state of being in the moment filled with the capacity and awareness to create and experience success. You no longer search solely for success in external experiences — such as a new job title, trendy automobile, increased paycheck and other external success trappings of traditional leadership. Instead, you combine your external success with internal awareness that provides access to the emotional and spiritual qualities you have yearned for so deeply.

SUCCESS IS YOUR NATURAL STATE

At this point in your leadership studies, you may be fully realizing that success, well-being, abundance and all other higher expressions of energy are your true nature. Your acceptance of this awareness is essential to experiencing maximized success. When you embrace this realization and accept that you already are that which you desire, you will become unstoppable.

Have you become so entrusted in using your energy to yearn for something you feel is outside of yourself that you lose track of your own current potential? It lives and vibrantly beckons from each experience encountered. Each moment is like a piece of clay waiting to be transformed into a beautiful piece of pottery.

As Inspired Authentic Leaders, you are ready to cast off the illusions and limitations of past beliefs and accept the success that thrives within, longing to be expressed. It is time to redirect your deepest fears and frustrations into the fuel for your forward momentum to start living within your fullest potential.

You are what you seek when you know that all the answers unfold within you"

You Are That Which You Seek

In the words of Saint Francis, "What we are looking for is what is looking." Rumi stated his awareness a bit differently, "What you seek is seeking you." Both quotes offer the inspiring belief, "You are that which you seek." Regardless of your desired experiences and qualities, each phrase elevates your self-awareness and helps you to embody the energy of the mastery leadership success state.

You have access to endless levels of potential thoughts, feelings, experiences, perceptions and intentions from which to create your success. You have an unlimited amount of possibilities that can be used to categorize and add color to your experiences. Therefore, the next time you find yourself wanting to experience more freedom in the workplace, remember that you don't have to wait. You can choose to tap into the energy and feelings associated with the experience of freedom without delay.

You no longer need to wait until some activity shows up that represents the type of experience you call freedom. There are many ways to experience your desired experiences without delay. When you become clear about your intentions, you speak words that generate these experiences, you look for evidence that your desire exists, and you learn to align your focus with the energy that supports each experience with your desired intentions.

In our time together, you have increased your awareness and identified your ideal vision of success. You've uncovered the part of you that knows who you need to become and why that goal is important. You have considered the success barometer that pinpoints the gap between where you are now and where you desire to go. This gap offers a decision point and the chance to pause, pivot and proceed toward the best path forward.

In the self-mastery section, you began to realize that you already have the energy and the success you strive for, even if your situation does not seem to reflect that in your current work life. You realize that in each moment you have access to the unlimited capacity to express yourself in any way you choose. Any success experience can be defined by one of the seven states of leadership success.

Consider the following summary of how experiences are managed effectively by using the leadership success state that applies to that situation.

- Greater levels of contribution are experienced within the leadership presence of the **cheerleader success state, #4**.

- Increased opportunity, partnerships and greater leadership potential are experienced in, the energy of the **opportunist success state, #5.**

- A sense of joy, creativity, inspiration and unity, can be experienced in the leadership presence of the **creator success state, #6,**

- Absolute passion, ultimate freedom and flow, are identified with the qualities and increased potential of the **self-mastery success state, #7.**

For each desired experience, there is an associated state of leadership success that aligns and defines you as an individual and as a leader of success.

The mastery leadership success state represents the Inspired Authentic Leader, which is the highest expression of success and home to your ideal vision of success. Although it is not possible to live in the mastery state long term, you now have the experience and connection to this state of being, and you can continue to expand your experience and connection with it. This is a state of being that is free from the illusion of limitations, it is filled with expansive and unlimited potential for increased success.

Regardless of the desire you wish to experience in your roles inside and outside your work day, you now have the awareness and increased potential to create any experience of success you choose. As a self-master, you realize that you are everything you could possibly desire. The potential and energetic capacity lives within you. All you need to do is embrace this energy and begin to "Rise and Shine" to new states of leadership and increased success.

ALL THE ANSWERS ARE WITHIN

This one phrase of awareness has been a beacon for me throughout my life, though it was a source of confusion in my early adulthood. When I was a young adult, I had a trusted friend I would often confide in, seek advice, share ideas and talk about life. There was one piece of advice I always remember, although it was sometimes a source of confusion and frustration. He always told me, "The answers are within you."

Each time I consulted him for some clarity, he repeated this phrase to me without giving much in the way of ideas to consider. Initially, as I reflected on the true meaning and potential of this phrase, I felt lost, unaware or somehow clueless as to what this adage might have to do with the current situation. As time passed, this phrase continued to sit at the back of my awareness. As I grew older it began to take on a rich deep meaning that has become one of the cornerstones of my life and my work with others.

I began to realize that each of us contains the answers to every single question we will ever ponder. As individuals, our questions will differ, therefore, so will the answers. What resonates true for me won't necessarily resonate true for you. That's the beauty of living in a society that is filled with human beings that are born with unique skills, perceptions, tendencies, ideas, insights and personal preferences. Our uniqueness builds strength in our society in its entirety.

The willingness to ask questions and trust our own instincts is often what's missing in our work lives. We are taught to show up to work in a robotic manner, and we are expected to respond to rituals and routines that leave us feeling little or no connection to our spiritual and emotional qualities that promote the feelings we most desire. We yearn to feel a deep sense of fulfillment, creativity, freedom, inspiration, contribution and impact.

Essentially, we are deprived of our greatest gifts to experience increased levels of success and expanded potential. This is the difference between traditional forms of leadership and authentic forms of leadership. Authenticity requires leaders to lead with self-awareness, including a greater connection to the phrase "the answers are within you." When we combine our intellectual insights with our creative intuitive abilities, we develop our own unique paths to becoming unstoppable and empowered to experience greater levels of success.

EMBRACING THE VOICE OF SUCCESS IN THE MIDST OF THE STORM

"I'm not afraid of storms, for I'm learning how to sail my ship."
- Louisa May Alcott

Have you ever heard the song titled, "Thunder" by Imagine Dragons? This song came to me during a very intense summer thunder storm while I was living in the Tampa Bay area of Florida, which is reported to be the lighting capital of North America. Each afternoon for several months, intense storms roll in, unleashing booming thunder, crackling lightning and torrential downpours. If you've never experienced a rainstorm of this caliber, trust me it can be quite unsettling. Even though you realize you are safe and secure inside a well-grounded building, the intensity of the storm is distracting, unnerving and sometimes frightening.

On one such day, I was working on an important project when a storm of greater intensity than most diverted my focus. I was completely distracted from my project and started to feel a little concern about when the storm would end. I realized the impact this experience was having on my mental, emotional, physical and spiritual self, so I decided to expand my awareness to connect with a greater perspective. As I explored new ways to align with the energy of this storm, I discovered the song "Thunder" by Imagine Dragons. It was a music genre that I would normally not pay much attention to, but somehow the spirit of the melody captured my attention and shifted my perspective on the event taking place. As the song played, I felt energetic and began to relax, sing along and feel empowered. This song transformed my energy and the experience I associated with thunderstorms.

As I searched for deeper awareness on the meaning and impact of these storms, I realized the lightning is the indicator and preparation for the impact to follow.

The lightning functions as a metaphor for the preparation and transformation of the actual event to take place. This awareness reminded me of our own power and potential for greatness that lives within each of us. Although the greatness exists within our capacity, it is often only reflected in subtle ways and may not be noticed, respected or acknowledged until it shows up with a big bang.

The thunder is the big bang that creates the explosion and commands attention. It's an example of the leader who is stepping up, speaking out and moving forward.

Thunder is symbolic to leadership and your ability to take ownership of your true potential and greatest opportunities to achieve success. It is the powerful, bold presence that steps forward to take inspired action. It is the difference between talking about a desire and making that desired experience happen, as well as fully enjoying its outcome. Embracing the thunder relates to uncovering your true potential for success. It is the powerful energy that resides within you, just waiting to be unleashed and enlivened with expression.

Thunder represents the bold actions you've taken in life and those that are yet to be taken. It is symbolic to stepping up, standing out and participating fully in life, which means seizing the opportunities of each new day.

As you reflect upon the power and energy of lightning and thunder, your awareness and definition will differ from mine. You have your own thoughts, associations and meaningful ways you relate to these two types of energy. There are many ways to embrace the energy and awareness of lightning and thunder as powerful metaphors for experiencing success. They can be representations for different states of being with various levels of intensity or experiences that contain both anabolic and catabolic energy that include periods of chaos as well as moments of silence that exist between the lightning and thunder activity.

The lightning is a phase of preparation that is necessary to prepare for the thunder that follows. Lightning can be startling, evoking tension and intensity, which in time will produce the powerful energy of the thunder. It opens the door for transformation to take place and the "big bang" that is to be released into the world.

The presence of lightning and thunder is truly a powerful metaphor to heeding the calls of your desires as they often sit idle beneath the surface of our awareness, creating subtle reminders that something is ready to transform. The presence of thunder is equally symbolic to your ability to take ownership of your core energy to create the experience you most deeply desire. It is your willingness to step beyond your comfort zone and embrace the awareness of "what wants to happen." It is the boldness to take inspired action that allows true transformation to occur.

As you embrace the potential of becoming the Inspired Authentic Leader and desire to create a leadership presence of self-mastery, you may choose to consider lightning as the indicator and awareness that echoes as the voice of change. Thunder is the impact and invitation to experience success, and the necessary transformation that needs to take place to embody your greatest potential.

Your experience of thunder might also invite you to embrace the flow between moments of chaos in comparison to the calm sunny days we prefer to experience. Just like the symbol of *Yin* and *Yang*, both complimentary energies are needed to complete the whole journey.

The *Yin* energy is the lightning, it is the indicator that something is wanting to happen, or an area of your life wants to change. It is the quiet, subtle, yet substantial sensation that waits beneath the surface ready to transform.

The *Yang* energy is the thunder. It represents the transformation that takes place to unleash the power and potential for our desired success.

Both energies are needed for the transformation to take place. The *Yin* energy of lightning is the catalyst; it is the pressure point that invites us to step outside our comfort zone, take risks and grow in new directions. The *Yang* energy of thunder is the transformation and the point of action that builds momentum. This type of energy embodies and embraces your full potential to expand your experiences and open the door to new opportunities to experience success.

The awareness of the lightning and the willingness to be the thunder offer messages of self-leadership and inspire us to show up fully. It's the perfect reminder of the greatness that resides within us and the opportunities that exist if we are receptive to them.

The lightning is the source of inspiration, the thunder is the call of the spirit, that steps forward, bold with grandness and greatness, and an unwillingness to sit quietly in the shadows of the clouds.

The boldness of the thunder resounds with an expanded awareness that is experienced in the state of self-mastery and the presence of the Inspired Authentic Leader.

Since the day of this intense storm and the new awareness I experienced, I now embrace the magic that takes place during a lightning and thunder storm. To me, these two energies are symbolic of our ability to listen for the subtle urges and sensations that sit beneath our awareness. This wisdom is combined with the opportunity to practice self-leadership through our willingness to step up and beyond our fears to be the thunder, a physical manifestation that rumbles in the skies to announce our greatest expressions of success.

As you consider the awareness offered and combine that with your own insights, I hope this shift in perspective will open the door for new potential the next time you experience a thundering moment of turbulence in your life. Consider allowing your next thunder-and-lightning episode to inspire you to acknowledge the messages residing within the unknown. Accepting those messages often leads to understanding and welcoming the exciting potential that is ready to erupt into the thunder state.

Embracing Your True Potential as The Inspired Authentic Leader

You have explored how to let go of illusions, blockages and resistance when the metaphoric rocks show up in the victim, dominance and status quo leadership success states. The energy and opportunities of these states are filled with catabolic, success-blocking energy. The lack of fulfillment and painful experiences that are experienced within these states function as an awareness, like the lightning discussed previously as an indicator of the thunder that is forthcoming.

Pain that is experienced in the lower states of leadership success can function as the catalyst that pulls you forward to experiencing your true potential. This pain is the friction discussed in the diamond that has been cut, crafted, and polished to its refined state. Your journey to becoming the Inspired Authentic Leader and the self-mastery state of success that you now experience is the reflection of your true leadership potential. Your leadership state is like the beauty of the diamond, formed under pressure, and then, exposed, cut and polished to reveal its core state of clarity, color, brilliance and value.

The Inspired Authentic Leader is a way of being that invites you to become your best self within every moment. It is a way to overcome the need to label experiences as wins or losses, good or bad, superior or inferior. You view each situation as an opportunity to experience life from a new perspective, free of judgment and open to the magic of the moment that fills you with a sense of freedom, deeper fulfillment, greater purpose, increased passion and limitless potential.

When you embody the qualities and characteristics of the Inspired Authentic Leader, you experience a wholeness within yourself that functions as a bridge between traditional leadership's "learned skills" and authentic leadership's "natural skills" that blend to catapult your success. You no longer struggle or resonate with the experience of suffering. Rather, you experience absolute power, creativity, freedom and increased fulfillment. Yes, there may be moments when you respond to challenges and difficult situations with either a victim, dominance or other catabolic leadership success state. However, these experiences are most often a temporary response. You now have the skills of self-mastery that will support you in transforming your energy, responses and reactions to a higher state of leadership success.

Going Beyond to Become the Greatness You Were Destined to Become

You now have a transformational tool based on the seven states of leadership success model. You can identify your current state of success in the moment and whether it supports you in creating success or results in limiting your success. This model can be used as a reference in support of choices, decisions and outcomes. It serves as a rule of clarity for who you will be in each moment and how you will show up in your work life.

You have the potential to direct your energy strategically for long-term sustainable success — regardless of how you define success or the vision of your desired outcome. If you use the seven states of leadership success model as a transformation tool, you can shift your energy toward higher states of success.

Just like using an automobile's navigation system to provide the fastest, most reliable paths to reach your destination, the seven states of leadership success model will keep you focused on your successful journey. You will have real-time feedback on the state of your energy, realizing when you are living and leading from a limited state of leadership and most likely feeling some form of lack, limitation, frustration, fear or narrow focus. As soon as you notice you have slipped into this less-than-desirable experience, you now have the awareness to shift your perspective and your behaviors to align with higher energies and strategies you have learned from the opportunist, creator and mastery leadership success states.

The seven states of leadership success model functions as your tool for creating success. Consider it your personal assistant guiding you toward your desired destination. You no longer live or lead from a place of uncertainty or distraction; you are laser-focused on creating and sustaining the success state you desire.

In the next chapter, you will find the way to create your unique formula for maximized success.

"Don't be afraid to give up the good to go for the great."

–John D. Rockefeller

19.
The Leader's Edge: Creating Your Unique Formula for Maximized Success

Together we have considered key aspects of success from many perspectives. We have explored several different methods to create and experience optimized and maximized success. We embraced the idea that the energy you use to create success is vital to determining if you become successful or if you remain stuck in a limited perspective.

As a leader, your primary energy drives your leadership performance in all aspects of life. This energy is always available to you, and it represents your full potential to create, experience and expand your success.

This energy fuels the formula to stack the cards in your favor by identifying your own unique formula for success. Your formula contains key factors that resonate with you and contribute to increased levels of success, helping you realize your goals.

Your formula for success establishes your ability to choose who you will be in each moment, how you will show up in the world and which states of success you will use to maximize your success.

As you review the key elements in your behaviors, thoughts, feelings and actions compared to their impact and the energetic qualities of each of your choices, you may benefit from setting aside quiet time to reflect on the questions that follow. Allocate time to ask the question and allow your inner wisdom and intuition to support you in completing your answers.

YOU ARE EMPOWERED TO CREATE YOUR OWN SUCCESS FORMULA

You have been empowered with the master transformation tool of the seven states of leadership success. Choose your state of success in each moment by asking the following questions:

- **Who am I being?**
  (What state of leadership success are you experiencing and expressing?)

- **How do I show up?**
  (What is the impact of your leadership presence for yourself and others?)

- **What is my state of success?**
  (Are you leading with success-building or success-blocking energy?)

You are fully empowered to choose how you will experience and express each of the seven states of leadership success. You have the capacity and increased awareness to know when to use each state and what to do if you find yourself living and leading from a success-blocking state instead of a success-building state. There may be times when you need to connect with others who reside in a success-blocking state to share their experience, so you are both able to communicate effectively. Your awareness and connection to all seven states of success has prepared you to assist others with understanding how to shift their energy and awareness to more productive states.

To uncover the core insights and potential that reside within the first few questions listed below, refer to the "what, why, how" formula that we explored in the self-leadership module to help you respond to each inquiry.

As you continue to craft your own unique formula for success, consider the following questions as a framework to stimulate thought and spark new insights and awareness.

Creating the Foundation of Self-Leadership

1. What Is Your Ideal Leadership Success State?
Bring your vision to life by mentally exploring each experience that comes up as you envision your ideal success state. Notice what you feel as a result of envisioning this state. What is different about your experience now? Which experiences contributed the most impact to your success? As you explore the vision of your success, spend some time in reflection, connecting with the energy of this desired experience and capture as much detail as possible. The more you experience the energy of your desired state, the more vivid and real it becomes.

2. What's Driving Your Vision?
What's the "why?" factor within this desire? Typically, it is not the physical or external goal you seek. Most often it's the feeling and the experience of that desire that drives and inspires your actions. Continue to ask yourself why something is important until your answers begin to repeat in consistency.

Putting Your Energy Into Action: Self-Management

3. Who Am I Being?
What practice will you put in place to help you identify and connect with your current state of being? As you increase your connection with your own state of being, we start to realize patterns of behaviors and default tendencies that either create success or inhibit success. These routine check-ins promote the opportunity to shift from lower states of being to higher states of being to ensure you are maximizing your success in each moment.

4. Success-Building or Success-Blocking-
Ask yourself, "What is the quality of my energy?" Are your actions currently mirroring more success-building or success-blocking energy? Come up with a fun plan using a timer as a reminder to check in and notice the quality of your energy. Or you may prefer creating a daily routine by quickly scanning your energy to notice which state you are experiencing. Practice the power of pause to scan your energy to assess its quality and overall potential to create success.

5. Responding versus Reacting-
Keep a journal of daily interactions that uncover situations when you notice yourself responding to situations and how you handled the situation effectively. Capture the beliefs, thoughts, feelings and associated responses that lead to your success. Also, record situations in which you were triggered to react rather than respond. It is helpful to keep a journal of your behavior patterns that lead to each reaction.

6. Your Energy Buster Plan-
Identify potential inspired actions you will take to free yourself from each of the four energy busters: limiting beliefs, assumptions, interpretations, inner critic. List the actions you will take each time you notice yourself experiencing one of the four energy busters. Include inspirations that you can reflect upon for renewed energy to help you move beyond any of the four energy busters.

7. Traditional versus Authentic Leadership-
How will you know if you are leading from a traditional leadership role perspective or an authentic leadership role perspective? Write a simple summary that defines you in each of the two perspectives, a traditional leadership presence and an authentic leadership presence. Refer to the self-management section to refresh yourself on the traits of each presence. Consider using images, words and other descriptors to illustrate your energy in each of the two perspectives so you can anchor your awareness on the different experience each role offers.

MAXIMIZING SUCCESS WITH SELF-MASTERY

8. **How will you measure your level of engagement?**
Reference the four levels of engagement referred to as the "DSCO model" in the self-mastery section. What inspired actions will you take during situations that exemplify drama and situation responses? How can you use this awareness to promote more alignment and leadership that is filled with choice and opportunity?

9. **What will you use to anchor the power of your choices?**
Will you use the coin theory as a reminder to look at multiple perspectives, recalling that each problem also includes a solution, or that each response can be shaped by the energies of drama and situation or by the energies of choice and opportunity? If the coin theory does not resonate with you, what method will you use as a reminder that "choice and opportunity" exist in the midst of the "drama and situation" experiences?

10. **Maximize Your Ability to Achieve Success**
Explore the potential of adding the energy of the six energetic success factors to maximize the potential of each opportunity. As you consider the potential impact of the physical, mental, emotional, spiritual, social and environmental energetic success factors, identify ideas about how to enhance each factor and how to overcome situations when the energetic factors are not in their optimal state. For example, you might choose one or two actionable items for each factor.

11. **Generating and Maintaining Higher Levels of Energy**
Consider putting together a self-mastery practice for incorporating the 5 R's of Success that was discussed in the self-mastery section. This plan of practice is used to generate and maintain higher levels of awareness and potential.

- What will I do to reignite my passion and experience a deeper sense of connection with myself and others?

- How will I renew my own success potential by increasing my ability to be present in the moment and utilize 100 percent of my power and presence in the moment?

THE EXPERIENCE OF BEING EXCEPTIONAL AS THE INSPIRED AUTHENTIC LEADER

12. Practice *Being* Success
How will you use the awareness of a super power figure to activate the energy of your success? Put together a vivid description of your desired experience. What super power resonates with you? When you are living and leading in this super-power state what's the overall experience?

13. Success is Your Natural State
How will you capture evidence that this statement is true for you? Each time you experience evidence of this statement, your belief and buy-in will intensify and deepen your connection to the energy that this statement provides. Creating a practice of self-reflection, meditation, and other activities offering opportunities to be still and reconnect to your own inner wisdom and awareness will help you deepen the understanding that "you are that which you seek" and "all the answers are within you." If you don't connect to this awareness, consider sitting in a quiet space and asking yourself, "What is the meaning of each of these phrases? What's the true potential if I did believe they were true?" Simply ask the question and be open to the answers you receive.

14. Combined Energy
How will I use the energy and awareness of the Inspired Authentic Leadership presence to connect with and inspire others?

15. The Success Generator Quick Reference

How can I use the awareness of the four-step process listed in the final pages of this chapter to activate my energy and generate increased levels of success in the moment?

Consider this structure when developing your own success formula. This formula provides you with a "leader's edge" to experiencing and sustaining optimal success. Your formula will differ from another person's formula. Use your creativity and inspiration to come up with ideas and insights that make your formula unique and one that is inspiring, actionable and provokes excitement.

You may decide to use each of the questions that I provided to stimulate ideas and insights for increased success, or you may choose only a few that resonate most strongly and provide the greatest momentum. Imagine you are a football coach who updates the team's playbook after each game. Your formula for success is designed to evolve and expand with new insights and wisdom that are meaningful to you as you move closer to experiencing your ideal vision of success.

20. The Combined Energy of Success Transforms the Workplace

You have taken the journey to becoming the Inspired Authentic Leader, a state of self-mastery that is highly skilled, aware and enlightened to embrace the potential for renewed states of success. It is now time to use this awareness to inspire and motivate others to increase their awareness and opportunities to excel beyond traditional forms of success. When you shift to the lower states of leadership, you experience isolation, limitation, loneliness and lack of support. The focus in these lower states of leadership is directed to self-success only and has little to no capacity for inspiring the success of others.

You have become accustomed to working in a self-fulfilling work life and have forgotten the core principles of nature to guide you toward abundance and increased success. When you look to nature, the true essence of your universe, you will notice animals that are most often in groups, or pairs and in some role of support. They understand the importance of combined potential, using each other's strength to help propel each other forward. As an example, consider the flock of geese flying effortlessly in a V-formation to maximize their energy and strength. Each bird instinctively knows how to align with the other birds. They seem to know instinctively when to turn left or right and when to slow or increase their speed. This simple flow of synchronicity and the oneness that is expressed by the geese formation is truly amazing. You never see one of the birds crash into the back of another; they all fly harmoniously with an ease and effortless momentum. Consider the laws of nature and the many examples it offers, and you will better understand the importance of synergy and combining your efforts with others.

Think about the principles of martial arts and how each practitioner uses combined energy, their own and the energy of their opponent. The Martial Arts Masters never resist the energy coming toward them, instead they transform the other person's energy to become a source of increased energy used for their own empowerment.

There are many natural occurrences offering evidence that working in a state of combined energy is more success-oriented than working solely for your own self-interest. Your combined energy is necessary to propel you individually and collectively toward greater success for all.

Your desire to connect, create and optimize your success using the higher states of leadership success clears your path to maximized success — individually, collectively and universally. When you honor the unique potential strengths of each person and release the judgment that isolates you, the workplace experience becomes filled with respect, integrity and enhanced experiences of success in all areas of the organization — top down, bottom up, inside, outside and beyond.

BECOMING A CATALYST FOR WORKPLACE SUCCESS

It's time to rise and shine, to be inspired, to be a catalyst for success and to be a vital member of a workplace transformation. This transformation is actually a movement that inspires leaders to take personal ownership of their work day, to discover their own true potential and to redefine their vision of workplace success.

Imagine what might be possible if you woke up each day with a desire for success and took personal responsibility for the energy you use to create your unique vision of success. As you increase your self-awareness and start to monitor the beliefs that drive your perceptions, thoughts, feelings and actions, you will notice which ones contribute the most potential toward your greatest success. Listen closely to the mental chatter, spiritual yearnings and any other internal and external factors to realize the hidden messages that are being conveyed to encourage you to become your best self.

What I am asking you to consider is a renewed state of being that reflects the qualities and characteristics of a self-mastery state that lives and leads from a place of inner peace and non-judgment. This renewed self-mastery state is enveloped in the spirit of allowing, with deeper levels of freedom, fulfillment and increased flow. This quest requires practice and a willingness to step into the unknown. It also requires trusting your own personal power and inner strengths to create higher states of success, regardless of the challenges presented.

NAMASTE` IN THE WORKPLACE

Another method for creating workplace success resides in your ability to offer respect and acknowledgment for each person's unique contribution. *Namaste`* is a yoga mantra and greeting that acknowledges mutual respect for each other. Its core meaning is "I honor the light that is within you that is also within me." This concept of honor, respect and partnership, in any form, has the potential to create synergy and increased opportunity to experience success. What might be possible if you utilize the energy of this mantra to foster the idea of *combined success*? How might this one simple gesture transform your workplace into increased engagement, with a sense of purpose and willingness to partner that overcomes the need to be dominating, self-focused and driven by lower states of leadership?

You don't have control over how others treat you, but you do have control over how you respond to each situation. You have the power to choose how you use your energy to create your experiences and, ultimately, your relationship to success. Once you realize that your power resides in each moment and that your experience of success depends on how you perceive each experience and respond to its potential, you will be able to choose the success you experience.

Throughout this book, the leadership success model has been discussed as a powerful skill that can be used to create increased levels of workplace success. However, this awareness doesn't stop at the end of the work day or work week. It is a vital resource for creating success in every role of your life - personally and professionally, locally and globally. This knowledge and awareness go well beyond the individual leadership role to promote renewed wisdom, insight and opportunities for coworkers, teams, programs, projects, organizations and corporations so they experience maximized success.

LEARNING TO WIN IN THE WORKPLACE

In this book, I have described a powerful vision and a strong passion for workplaces that are filled with empowered leaders. They are inspired with the self-mastery qualities reflected in the presence of the Inspired Authentic Leader. These leaders embody a vision for each work-related experience to be one of artistry, impact, contribution and increased connection. The ability to win exists within the parameters of each moment; it is not measured by the digits that appear in your paycheck following the latest raise in salary.

That said, it is healthy to embrace the traditional elements that come along with striving to stay in the winning column in the workplace. It is also important to ensure that you experience the rewards from the internal success — feeling inspired, engaged, excited, motivated, fulfilled, creative, purposeful and impactful. These feelings spark the sensations that keep you vibrant and truly connected to your own vision of workplace success. Winning in the workplace is no longer an illusion but a true sense of purpose. Workplace winners are impassioned and aligned with increased potential for optimal success.

As you begin to put the information you have learned into action, consider the following four-step quick reference for generating success. These four steps will help you lead from your highest success states, which is why I refer to this process as a "success generator." The following questions and related guidance provide a brief summary of our work together. Consider the questions listed below to anchor your energy and awareness into your optimal success-oriented potential.

The Success Generator
QUICK REFERENCE

#1 AWARENESS -
What Wants to Happen?

Demonstrate your ability to show up as a leader, live in the moment, ask "What wants to happen?" and listen to each response. Inside pure awareness and true success, there is no predetermined outcome, label or judgment. You are committed to discovery and open to the energy of success in each moment.

#2 BEING -
Who Am I Being?

Rely on your willingness to embrace a presence of success in the way you show up and how you respond to each experience. Embrace the states of leadership success and all their expressions; including joy, peace, ease, creativity, inspiration, confidence and authenticity.

#3 ALIGNMENT -
Are My Thoughts, Feelings and Actions
in Alignment with Success?

Know when your actions are potentially success-building or success-blocking? Align your behavior and daily responses with your desired intentions. This activity ensures that you maintain your focus on your goals and ensure that you direct your energy toward a productive and success-oriented vision.

#4 PARTNERSHIP -
Do I Maintain Balance?

Combine the awareness of "who you are being" with "what you are doing." This internal partnership guides your external actions, helping you create success that is deeply impactful and purposeful.

We have covered a lot of information in every chapter of this book. Sometimes figuring out how to implement the core nuggets of awareness can seem overwhelming and even frustrating at times. When you use the four condensed inspired-action steps, you will be anchored in awareness of the information we have explored together. If you use these steps as a quick reference for inspired actions, you will be well on your way to ensuring that you enjoy the greatest potential for maximizing your success.

In the last chapter, you are invited to enjoy being the Inspired Authentic Leader who experiences maximized success and helps other leaders achieve that empowering sense of success as well.

This is your time to *"rise and shine!"*

21. Inspired Authentic Leaders – It's Your Time to Rise and Shine!

This is your call to action!
The information provided in this book will support you in creating your desired experience of increased success. Together, we have taken an enlightening and personal journey to help you discover your greatest potential for leadership success inside and outside the workplace. The transformational tools that will impact and enhance your leadership success are always available to you in the sections on the seven leadership success states.

> *"Our greatest ability as humans is not to change the world; but to change ourselves."*
> *- Mahatma Gandhi*

I am passionate about inspiring you to unleash the Inspired Authentic Leader who already lives within you. My goal is to ignite within you a deep understanding of the potential that exists in the presence of the Inspired Authentic Leader.

Now it is time for you to take this spark of inspiration and share it with others. Leverage this catalyst to positively impact the teams, groups, projects, organizations and corporations where you work and lead. You are empowered to offer this body of wisdom and awareness to generate a new era for workplace success. The vision of the Inspired Authentic Leader is one of success that far exceeds the limitation of traditional leadership success. It is a vision of success filled with the energy of freedom, deeper fulfillment, and a sense of purpose that flows effortlessly with confidence and mutual respect, and it is **only experienced at the expanded states of leadership success.**

When you realize that you are, by nature, a success-oriented individual, the struggle only shows up when you stop *being* success! Your success unfolds naturally once you realize you *are* the presence of success. Then, and only then, do you become the amazing leaders you were destined to become.

THE OPPORTUNITY

The Inspired Authentic Leader is a leadership presence that unleashes the purpose, passion and increased potential of every leader, every organization, and every corporation that yearns to live and lead with the energy of being unstoppable. We are designed to embrace the absolute greatest experience of going above and beyond to be exceptional. The Inspired Authentic Leader embodies the spirit of workplace success, and it carries the potential for limitless success with unstoppable power and an impact that is profound.

It is now your time to "Rise and Shine" so you can be the leader you've always desired to become. I leave you to respond to your call to action with a final thought to always remember.

*There is a unique, enlightened and empowered
leader within you, like an exotic blossom
that is waiting and wanting to bloom.*

Within you lies the power of success, alive and vibrant. Use this awareness to bloom into a masterful leader who is powerfully and energetically unstoppable!

To Your Success, with Love and Compassion,

Donna Tarquinio

Special Invitation to Partner

Becoming an Inspired Authentic Leader with boundless success is an exhilarating and ongoing journey into Self-Mastery Leadership. After reading this book, if you yearn for deeper levels of authentic success but you're not sure where to start, please contact me to explore our potential partnership.

If you wish to know more about how to apply the techniques offered or want a guide to lead you forward to maximizing your success, I would be delighted to support you on your journey and help you achieve the success your heart desires.

This book provides a roadmap for my programs, workshops and coaching services for individuals, groups and corporations. It would be an honor to hear from you and share thoughts on your journey toward becoming unstoppable.

Please visit our website at www.beyondstatusquo.com or contact me directly at donna@beyondstatusquo.com

Notes:

Notes:

Notes:

www.ingramcontent.com/pod-product-compliance
Lightning Source LLC
Chambersburg PA
CBHW042113100526
44587CB00025B/4034